THE COMPLETE
Small Claims
Handbook
for NEW YORK STATE

Know the Process—
Win Your Case

THOMAS D. GIORDANO
DANIEL A. GIORDANO

Looseleaf
Law Publications, Inc.

43-08 162nd Street • Flushing, NY 11358
www.LooseleafLaw.com • 800-647-5547

Library of Congress Cataloging-in-Publication Data

Giordano, Thomas D.
    The complete small claims handbook for New York State: know the process, win your case / Thomas D. Giordano and Daniel A. Giordano.
        p. cm.
    Includes bibliographical references and index.
    ISBN 978-1-60885-027-3
  1. Small claims courts--New York (State) I. Giordano, Daniel A. II. Title.
    KFN5976.G567 2011
    347.747'04--dc23

                                        2011021907

Cover by *Sans Serif, Inc.* Saline, Michigan

Table of Contents

To my parents, Frank and Carmela Giordano

T.D.G.

About the Authors

Thomas D. Giordano is a full time Associate Professor of Business Law at the College of Professional Studies of St. John's University in Jamaica, New York. He earned a Juris Doctor degree from St. John's University School of Law and an accounting degree from St. John's University. He holds law licenses in New York, New Jersey and Florida, and is admitted to the United States District Court (New York Eastern and Southern Districts). Professor Giordano was recognized by the Chief Judge of the State of New York for his outstanding service as a Nassau County District Court small claims arbitrator. He also has served as a hearing officer for New York State Supreme Court and arbitrator for the New York Stock Exchange, American Arbitration Association, Better Business Bureau, and trial courts in Queens and Suffolk Counties. Currently, he arbitrates civil cases for Nassau County District Court and securities matters for Financial Industry Regulatory Authority Dispute Resolution. Professor Giordano's writings include law review and bar journal publications and a supplement to a widely-used college business law text.

Daniel A. Giordano is a teacher of English literature who received his B.A. degree *summa cum laude* from Loyola University Maryland, where he was a Presidential scholar. Mr. Giordano is a member of Sigma Tau Delta, the International English Honor Society that recognizes distinguished work in English language and literature.

Introduction

A s a college law professor and small claims arbitrator, I have had cause to evaluate the state of America's high school graduates' legal knowledge and the quality of the presentations of small claims litigants. Sadly, the American educational experience excludes a thorough study of our laws. The example of high school driver education courses, wherein students are instructed on traffic law, is notable for its uniqueness. It seems that notions about law held by many Americans are acquired from independent reading, news and entertainment media, and life experiences. In both the classroom and the courtroom, I have seen that this approach leaves many of our citizens somewhat less informed about our laws than they might be.

People involved in ordinary litigation rely on attorneys to know the relevant law and procedure. In small claims cases, people generally represent themselves because attorney fees would be disproportionate to the recovery. Their legal knowledge and preparedness, therefore, can be the difference between winning and losing. The more law a small claims litigant knows and the more prepared she is, the more likely she will be to properly evaluate the strengths and weaknesses of her case, to properly assess whether to proceed, and to prevail if she does proceed. In this book I explain the fundamental legal principles relevant to many small claims and the procedures followed in court. I also include a chapter on alternatives to court action. With an eye toward the reality that a small claim does not amount to the proverbial "federal case," I have tried to cover the subject matter comprehensively without prolixity. I have drawn on my experiences in small claims court, law practice, and legal education to prepare what I hope is a valuable guide to all persons involved with small claims. Greater knowledge and better advocacy increase the probability of justice for all, which ultimately is the goal of the rule of law.

Thomas D. Giordano

"Fairness is really what justice is."

– Associate Justice Potter Stewart,
United States Supreme Court[1]
(1915-1985)

"The good judge is not he who does hair-splitting justice to every allegation, but who, aiming at substantial justice, rules something intelligible for the guidance of suitors."

– Ralph Waldo Emerson[2]
(1803-1882)

See endnotes – page 81

iv

Chapter 1

Scope and Objectives

Guides for persons attempting to resolve minor disputes are readily available, and scholarly articles on the laws and court procedures relating to such disputes have been published. This book is meant to combine the themes of both in one resource. Guidance for laymen pursuing small claims justice is juxtaposed with New York law relevant to small claims actions. Statutes, case law, and court rules are cited in extensive endnotes for the benefit of judges, arbitrators, attorneys, and laymen.

Laws are rules created by federal, state, and local governments. Because both the rules of court procedure and most of the law used to resolve small claims derive from state law, they will vary across the country. For example, the amount of money that is recoverable in court will vary, as will the filing fees. No effort is made in this book to present the law of any state other than New York, but to the extent that other states may have similar laws, the book will be helpful to persons in those states. The general information that I have included on properly preparing and presenting a case in court should prove beneficial to any small claims litigant.

Throughout the State of New York, small claims are heard in a special *part*, called the small claims part, of four different trial courts – New York City Civil Court (in New York City), District Court (in Nassau County and parts of Suffolk County), City Court (in cities other than New York City), and Justice Court (elsewhere in the state). There is no court in New York State officially named "Small Claims Court"; however, throughout this book these small claims parts usually will be referred to as *small claims court* for the sake of simplicity. Small claims actions in each of these trial courts are governed by a separate set of laws that includes a statute ("Court Act") and court rules ("Uniform Rules") for the trial court. Most, but not all, of the provisions of the laws and rules for the four trial courts are identical. Unless otherwise noted, all references in this book to Court Act and Uniform

Rules will be to the New York City Civil Court Act[3] and Uniform Civil Rules for the New York City Civil Court.[4] If you are litigating outside of New York City, you should consult the Court Act and Uniform Rules for the court in which you will appear.[5] The Court Act and Uniform Rules are covered in detail in Chapter Seven. Although they receive less emphasis, commercial claims also are addressed in this book. These are claims that may be brought by business entities in accordance with rules similar to those governing ordinary small claims.

To win any court case, a litigant must present his arguments and evidence in accordance with the court's procedures (procedural law) and must persuade the judge or jury that according to the relevant rules of law (substantive law) as applied to the facts proved in the case, his position is the right one. For example, if it is proved by eyewitness testimony (admissible evidence under procedural law) that while driving a vehicle, Mr. Smith passed a red traffic light and collided with Mr. Suarez, then Mr. Smith will be found responsible for the collision since the relevant state statutory law (substantive law) prohibits Mr. Smith's actions.

In preparing to try a case, a lawyer attempts to familiarize himself with all of the relevant substantive law. In a simple case, the lawyer may already know the law, but in a more complicated case she may have to conduct research. In the same way, a small claims litigant should make every attempt to learn the substantive law pertaining to her case. For anyone without a law school education that could be a daunting task. Fortunately, most small claims disputes involve simple rules of law. Non-lawyers may often learn all they need to know by reading self-help books or through basic legal research. In more complicated cases, an attorney's advice may be necessary. To assist our readers, technical terms used in this book that appear in bold type constitute a glossary included as an appendix for easy reference.

Some basic substantive law concepts typically applied to resolve small claims are covered in Chapters Three and Four. Guidance is given in Chapter Five for those persons who might want to research the law in more detail at their local libraries or via the Internet. A brief warning is appropriate here. Because most laws and discourses on law are written by lawyers or for lawyers and judges, or both, they are often confusing to non-lawyers. Consequently, laymen risk wasting time reading irrelevant laws and misinterpreting legal writings. Anyone researching law must take great care to focus on the relevant law and to find ALL of it because the *one* exception to the rule that is not discovered may be the one that determines the case.

The simple procedures that must be followed in small claims actions, described in Chapter Seven, are easy to understand; however, litigants routinely lose cases when they do not familiarize themselves with those procedures. For example, claimants lose property damage cases when they fail to submit the specific evidence sufficient to establish the extent of damage and necessity of repair work; namely, an itemized paid bill for repairs made, or two itemized estimates of necessary work. Some of the more complex rules of evidence are noted in that chapter, but they rarely are decisive in small claims cases.

In short, this book is a substantive and procedural law guide for laymen and lawyers in New York State, with specific reference to New York City Civil Court small claims actions but generally applicable to all New York small claims. Readers of this book will learn about the legal rights and obligations of consumers, business persons, and others, be better able to assess chances for success if involved in a dispute, and be better prepared to resolve a dispute by settlement or legal proceeding.

Finally, the feminine and masculine genders of pronouns have been used randomly throughout the book with intent to represent them equally. Each is deemed to include the other and the neuter gender as appropriate.

Chapter 2

Determining Whether
Small Claims Legal Action
Is Appropriate for the Dispute

Small claims courts dispense affordable justice to many people; however, the following facts about the court make it an inappropriate choice for dispute resolution in some cases. In typical cases, the only remedy available in small claims court is money damages. The geographic area in which the court has power is very limited. Illegal behavior will be addressed; immoral or unfriendly behavior will not. Court judgments ordering the payment of money are not self-executing. Consequently, a person involved in a dispute must carefully analyze it and evaluate her chances of achieving a satisfactory outcome before suing in small claims court. The outcome depends upon factors examined in this chapter: the remedy sought, the relevant substantive and procedural laws, the degree of harm suffered, the location of the person to be sued, called the *defendant*, and the likelihood of obtaining payment from him. Sometimes the dispute resolution alternatives described in Chapter Six yield better results.

DETERMINE WHETHER THE LOCAL SMALL CLAIMS COURT HAS AUTHORITY OVER THE DEFENDANT

The power of a small claims court to hear a case against a particular defendant is severely limited. The law permits an action against a small claims defendant only in the location that is convenient for her, without regard to whether it is convenient for the person suing, who is called the *claimant* or *plaintiff*. The action may be maintained only where the defendant lives, works, or has a business office. These limitations are detailed in Chapter Seven. Consequently, a claimant may have to choose between forbearance and litigation in a distant county or state. If a claimant attempts to sue a defendant in the wrong location, the claim will be rejected by court personnel at the outset.

DETERMINE WHETHER THE CASE IS WINNABLE

Victory in court depends on whether the claimant proves by a preponderance of evidence that:

1. the claimant has suffered compensable harm (*damage*);
2. the defendant caused such harm by committing a legal wrong (*liability*); and
3. the court has power to grant the remedy sought by the claimant.

These matters are covered in detail in Chapters Three, Four, and Seven. Following is an overview of the topic.

Preponderance of evidence refers to the claimant's *burden of proof* and means that she must offer more admissible, credible evidence establishing the basis for victory than the defendant offers. The admissibility of evidence is determined by the judge or arbitrator in accordance with applicable procedural law. Generally, some evidence other than the claimant's own testimony is needed to carry this burden. The simple reason for this is that if both the claimant's and defendant's testimonies are equally credible, though inconsistent, there is a tie between them as to evidence, and the defendant must prevail because the claimant will not have offered *more* credible evidence than the defendant. Thus, the adage that the claimant cannot win if the case comes down to his word against the defendant's word usually is true. If, however, the claimant's testimony is credible and the defendant's is not, then the claimant may prevail without further evidence. Evidence may include the testimony of supporting witnesses (including expert witnesses), photographs, documents, audiotape, videotape, physical evidence such as defective or damaged property, paid bills, estimates, medical records, and many other things that help prove a case.

The claimant's evidence must prove facts, which within the context of the law establish liability and damages. These are the twin requirements for proving a cause of action and winning a case. The term *damages* refers to the compensation due under law for the harm suffered. A claimant must prove that she has suffered legally compensable harm to establish the damages portion of her case. Not all harm, however, is compensated through court action. For example, neither inconvenience experienced nor time expended in preparing a court case is compensable. Compensable harm is determined according to the type of case. It may include such losses as medical expenses incurred, pain and suffering experienced, wages lost, enjoyment of life lost due to physical injury, loss in value of or cost to repair damaged property, and other financial loss.

The term *liability* refers to the responsibility imposed by law upon one person for another's damages caused by the commission of a legal wrong. The victim to whom the wrongdoer is liable is entitled to certain remedies in civil court. When used generically, the term *civil court* refers to any court that decides non-criminal cases. The legal wrongs that result in the imposition of liability are in the form of either **breach of contract**, causing financial loss to the other contracting party, or the inflicting of harm on another person or her property in a way prohibited by law, referred to as **tort**.

When a person breaks promises that are part of an agreement recognized under law as a contract, she probably is committing breach of contract. For example, if Aunt Hilda promised to pay $50.00 to her neighbor in exchange for her neighbor's used lawnmower but failed to do so, Aunt Hilda would have committed a legal wrong by breaching the contractual agreement with her neighbor. If, however, Aunt Hilda promised to give $50.00 to her niece for her birthday but failed to do so, Aunt Hilda would have committed no legal wrong because her promise was not part of a contractual agreement.

Under tort law, the harm that befalls someone may be the fault of the person himself, the fault of others, a combination of the two, or no one's fault. In the first and last instances, generally there is no liability on anyone's part. In the other two instances, if there is a law addressing the behavior involved, a legal wrong is committed and liability is imposed on the wrongdoer. In those two instances, if the victim has suffered compensable harm, he will be permitted to pursue a cause of action against the alleged wrongdoer. For example, if a person trips on his own untied shoelaces, no legal wrong is committed against him. If a person is knocked down by a gust of wind, no legal wrong is committed against him. But if a person trips in part or entirely because of an uneven sidewalk, the person responsible for maintaining the sidewalk may have committed a legal wrong against him. Certain conduct, such as striking another person, exposes the actor to both criminal prosecution and civil (tort) liability. Only the civil liability aspects are discussed in this book.

Knowing the relevant law of liability and damages in breach of contract and tort cases informs a person as to the nature of the evidence the judge or arbitrator will expect in a given case and enables her to make an educated guess as to whether she will prevail. The concepts of liability and damages are detailed in Chapters Three and Four.

Each civil court is empowered to grant some or all of the specific judicial remedies that fall into two distinct classes: remedies at law and remedies in equity. The ordering of one person to pay another a sum of money is the most commonly granted law remedy, and it is granted by courts whenever it is adequate to do justice. When money judgments are inadequate, certain civil courts are empowered to grant the more unusual equitable remedies, such as injunctions or orders to perform contracts. Small claims courts are authorized by law to grant only money judgments in ordinary cases; they have no power to grant other remedies except to persons aggrieved by certain arbitration awards.[6] If a person will be satisfied with a court order entitling him to a sum of money from the alleged wrongdoer, then small claims court is an option for his dispute. If, however, a person seeks any other kind of court order, he will find small claims court unable to accommodate him even if he can establish liability.

The maximum money a New York small claims court may award in any case, exclusive of interest and court costs, is $5,000.00,[7] except in the Justice Courts where the maximum is $3,000.00.[8] Cases potentially worth substantially more than those amounts probably should not be brought in small claims court since recovery would be limited to the jurisdictional maximum. Such cases may justify the additional cost of attorney fees usually associated with higher-level court proceedings. Sometimes it is easy for a claimant to know the amount of money to which she would be legally entitled upon court victory. For example, if a $500.00 bill for services rendered has not been paid, the proper award to a prevailing claimant would be $500.00, plus interest and costs. Other times, it is not so simple. Most notably, personal injury cases are harder to quantify and probably require an experienced attorney's evaluation.

DETERMINE WHETHER THE DEFENDANT EITHER IS INSURED OR FINANCIALLY ABLE TO PAY A JUDGMENT

The probability of the satisfaction of a judgment is the single most important issue to be addressed in determining whether court action is appropriate, unless a claimant would happily accept a Pyrrhic victory. Most often, collection is the foremost concern of litigation attorneys when they begin to evaluate any case because victory is pointless if the judgment debtor is not insured and does not have reachable assets for satisfaction of the judgment. Various laws create procedures to collect judgments but they are ineffectual if the losing defendant is *judgment proof*, meaning without assets that are reachable under law for payment. Some defendants have few assets; others have significant assets that are not reachable under law. The latter scenario is playing out in the famous California wrongful death civil case against the former football player, O.J. Simpson.[9] The plaintiffs in that case have collected little or none of the more than thirty-three million dollars awarded them by court judgment because Mr. Simpson's assets are beyond the reach of his judgment creditors. This topic is covered in detail in Chapter Seven.

Chapter 3

Breach of Contract Cases

Illegal acts come in three forms in the United States. Crimes are public wrongs prosecuted by the people through their representatives in government (e.g., District Attorney and United States Attorney), the consequences for which include incarceration and fines. The other two forms of illegal acts are the private wrongs known as breaches of contract and torts. Victims of these wrongs may sue alleged wrongdoers in court, most often seeking money damages. These wrongs are described as private rather than public since the consequences of the wrongs are less likely to affect the general public in the way that crimes do. The private wrongs are also referred to as *civil* wrongs, and they are litigated in the *civil* courts. Both types of private wrongs may be redressed in small claims court. In this and the next chapter, these terms will be thoroughly defined and examples of typical breach of contract and tort claims litigated in small claims court, will be offered with an examination of the applicable law.

LIABILITY

Contract law largely has been created by our courts as part of the process of making decisions in cases involving private agreements. A cornerstone of contract law is that promises included in contractual agreements deserve legal enforcement. A contractual agreement, or contract, is an agreement (indicated by written evidence in special cases where a law called the **statute of frauds** requires it) to which competent persons have genuinely consented, provided it is made for a lawful purpose and is supported by consideration. Breach of contract is the legal wrong that arises from a failure to fulfill a duty created by contractual agreement. The failing or breaching party is said to be liable, or legally responsible, to the victim of the breach for foreseeable harm caused, and he must compensate the victim with money in an amount equal to the harm. To establish liability a plaintiff must prove that she had a contract with the defendant and that the defendant breached it. If the defendant argues that the claimant breached the contract, the claimant must be prepared to refute that allegation as well.

Establish the Existence of a Contract

Agreements that are enforceable in court as described above are accomplished either through oral or written communication or by deliberate interaction of the parties, without words of agreement. The former are called express contracts and the latter, implied-in-fact contracts or implied contracts. People make oral contracts and implied contracts regularly without thinking in those terms. Many agreements for the purchase and sale of services or inexpensive merchandise are either oral or implied contracts. For example, an oral agreement between neighbors to buy and sell a used lawn mower for $100.00 is an enforceable oral contract. Similarly, a typical transaction between restaurant and customer is viewed under law as an implied contract because the deliberate interaction of the parties shows their implied agreement to sell and buy the restaurant's food and service. Notice that the parties involved in the typical restaurant transaction do not actually speak or write their agreement with each other. Customers never actually say they will pay the bill, and the restaurant employees never actually promise to do anything. Their intentions and promises are inferred from the way they interact with each other in a particular setting. For legal purposes, however, the resulting contract is every bit as real and legally binding as a fifty-page signed document!

Breach of contract cases involving written contracts are simpler to resolve because the promises of the parties are in writing and generally cannot be denied. The terms of some written contracts are thoroughly negotiated by the parties, their attorneys, or both, and in other cases, pre-printed form contracts are presented in a take-it-or-leave-it manner. The documents generally are the only evidence needed to establish both the existence of a contractual agreement and the exact promises exchanged. Typically, court cases turn either on the quality of performance of contractual duties by one of the parties or the interpretation of contract language. A careful review of all contract language is essential to the determination of the parties' rights. Often a judge or arbitrator will seize upon a clause or a single word in the contract to decide the case.

Oral and implied agreements are not always considered contractual agreements. There is a group of laws in every state collectively referred to as the statute of frauds that require a showing of some signed, written evidence of the agreement before it will be enforced in court if the agreement is in a protected class. Important types of agreements in the protected classes include agreements involving most real property transactions,[10] sales of products with a price of $500.00 or more,[11] and agreements that cannot possibly be completed within one year from the time they are made.[12] A party to any such agreement must be sure to obtain some evidence of the agreement in writing, signed at least by the other party. The written evidence need not take the form of a complete written contract, but the evidence should refer to the deal, including description of the subject matter and quantity in a product transaction, identification of the parties, and price. Without such written evidence a claimant probably will not prevail over an adversary's objections in small claims litigation. Of course, even when an oral or implied agreement is enforceable without a writing (i.e., not in a protected class), a claimant alleging breach must prove by a preponderance of the evidence that such an agreement actually was made. Often this is difficult or impossible if the defendant denies the allegations since the claimant may have no evidence other than his own word.

The other parts of the definition of contractual agreement rarely are disputed in small claims litigation; therefore, they are only summarily addressed here. The reference to competent persons limits the power to make contracts to persons with enough mental ability to know what a contract is and to understand the obligations involved. Excluded from this class are all underage persons, known as **infants** or minors, and persons who are **incompetent** due to mental deficiency. State law determines the age at which infancy ends; in New York it is eighteen for most purposes.[13] An agreement entered into by an infant or incompetent person generally is not considered a valid contract and is not legally binding upon that person.[14]

The part of the definition referring to genuine consent requires non-enforcement by the courts if one party is physically forced, unduly influenced, or defrauded into making an agreement.[15] Certain serious mistakes about the facts that both parties relied on in making an agreement also invalidate the consent.[16] These issues are rarely litigated because their legal meanings are very strictly drawn leaving their relevance unlikely. Most agreements involve lawful purposes; however, certain contracts are treated as unlawful where one party does not have the required governmental licensing. New York State law specifically prohibits unlicensed home improvement contractors, catering establishments, and electronic or home appliance service dealers from maintaining court actions for payment for services rendered if any local law requires licensing.[17]

Most agreements are supported by consideration, which is the legal term for something of value. The consideration requirement limits contractual agreements to actual bargains of exchange.[18] One-way transactions, such as promised gifts are distinguished from contractual agreements. Since most people expect to give-and-take in business transactions with other persons, virtually all commercial agreements include consideration. If, however, a claimant is alleging that a defendant failed to keep her promises, but the defendant is that rare person who demanded and received nothing for those promises, then lack of consideration is an argument for the defendant to make in the case. To make the existence of consideration eminently clear, drafters of written contracts often include the phrase, "for one dollar and other good and valuable consideration, the parties agree as follows," or words to that effect.

Establish That the Defendant Breached the Contract

Small claims breach of contract cases typically boil down to whether or not the defendant kept his part of the bargain. Defendants often argue that they committed no breach because they fulfilled all their contractual promises. They might argue that plaintiffs are misinterpreting the contract, have unreasonable expectations about the quality of work or goods, or simply are not being truthful. Since the burden is on the plaintiff to prove her case, she must be ready to counter any such arguments with solid evidence, such as photographs, testimony of witnesses, or a paid bill or two estimates showing the need to redo or repair the defendant's work.

Establish That the Claimant Did Not Breach the Contract

It may become necessary for the claimant to show that she did fulfill her contractual obligations or that she was at all times ready to do so. Claimants who allege breach of contract often are accused by defendants of not fulfilling their own promises. The defendant then argues that his promised performance was excused because of the claimant's breach. For example, a homeowner who is accused of not paying a house painter in full might justify the underpayment by alleging that the house painter breached the contract first by not painting the trim. In that case it would be critical for the house painter-claimant to show that he fulfilled all of his contractual duties.

Other Law Affecting Liability

Sales Law

The statutory law of sales applies to transactions in goods (roughly the equivalent of products) and includes many provisions that differ from the contract law rules applicable to other transactions. If a small claim involves the sale of goods, the claimant would be wise to check the relevant statute, the

Uniform Commercial Code,[19] for any provision applicable to his claim. Some of the more important provisions are the *firm offer rule*,[20] *sale of goods statute of frauds*,[21] and the *implied warranty* provisions.[22]

According to basic contract law, a business agreement is considered made when the party to whom an offer is extended properly notifies the other of his acceptance of it. Contract law generally allows the offering party to withdraw her offer any time before the other party accepts it. The firm offer rule, however, provides that if a party who deals in goods (**"merchant"**) offers by a signed writing to contract with another party for goods, promising in the writing to allow the other party some time to decide whether to accept the offer, the merchant is bound by his promise. The merchant is not permitted to withdraw the offer during the promised time, up to a period of three months. For example, if a car salesman offered on dealership letterhead to sell Mr. Winston a certain car for $25,000.00, "if Mr. Winston agrees within 3 days," then the salesman would be required by law to honor the offer during those three days.

The sale of goods statute of frauds provides that no contract for the sale of goods with a price of $500.00 or more will be enforceable in court without written evidence thereof signed by the person accused of breach.[23] Consequently, oral and implied agreements for such goods generally may not form the basis for a breach of contract action; however, the following exceptions to this rule are noteworthy.

Even without the requisite writing, agreements will be enforceable to the extent any payment for or delivery of goods has been made,[24] or if the defendant openly admits the existence of the contract.[25] Thus, if two persons make a handshake deal for the purchase and sale of a particular used car for $500.00 and the seller reneges, the buyer will have no legal recourse, even if he can produce witnesses to the handshake deal, unless the buyer can prove that he paid part of the price or the defendant admits in court the making of the handshake deal. In the latter two events, the buyer would be permitted to proceed with his case.

A much narrower exception applies only to transactions between merchants. This exception leaves the requirement of written evidence in place but eliminates the requirement that it be signed by the alleged breaching party. The exception applies in cases where the breaching merchant previously received the writing from the other party as confirmation of an oral agreement and did not object to it as such within ten days.[26] It works as follows: if both the buyer and seller of the car in the previous scenario were automobile dealers and one sent a signed written confirmation of the handshake deal to the other who did not timely object to its contents, such writing could be used to support a breach of contract case against either party who might breach. Under the general rule, it could be used against the one who signed it and under the exception it could be used against the one who failed to object.

The final exception states that if the agreement is for custom-made goods and the seller has begun manufacture, the writing requirement is eliminated.[27]

Warranties imposed by law relating to the quality of goods have revolutionized contract law for sales of goods. Most notably, in all sales of goods by merchants, modern law implies a warranty that the goods are fit for ordinary use.[28] This warranty, called the implied warranty of merchantability, becomes part of the sale whether or not the merchant seller actually makes such a statement. Sales of goods are no longer transactions where the law warns, "Let the buyer beware." The warranty of merchantability is so far-reaching that it is almost impossible to remember or imagine what commerce was like without it. Before the merchantability warranty, buyers of goods had little or no legal recourse if the goods were defective. The burden was almost entirely on them to inspect before purchase and determine for themselves if the goods were of adequate quality. Today's consumers routinely bring merchandise back to retailers when they believe it to be defective, and they expect the merchants to replace it or refund the purchase price. Their expectations often are met because of goodwill and because of the seller's familiarity with the implied warranty of merchantability. Remember, however, that the warranty only applies if the sale was made by a seller considered to be a merchant.

Often, consumers and merchants are confused about the interplay between a seller's refund policy and the warranty of merchantability. The warranty applies to cases where the goods are defective in some way, and it overrides any refund policy. If the goods are defective and the seller had not disclaimed the implied warranty (e.g., by making the sale "as is"), the buyer may return the goods, and the seller must make an appropriate adjustment regardless of any refund policy to the contrary. Refund policies generally govern when the consumer simply desires to return non-defective merchandise for personal reasons. Then the consumer has whatever rights the policy bestows, or where no policy is conspicuously posted, the right to receive a cash refund or store credit, at her option, if the return is made within thirty days of purchase.[29]

Agency Law

An *agent* is a person authorized by another person, called his *principal*, to act on the principal's behalf. Agents often are used to accomplish business transactions. For example, insurance agents act on behalf of insurance companies, sports agents on behalf of athletes, and salesmen on behalf of their employers. When one person or company uses an agent to enter into transactions with others called *third parties*, the agent's actions legally bind the principal in contract. If the agent signs a contract with a third party on behalf of his principal, the contract really is between the principal and the third party. The agent is not a party to the contract but is treated legally as if he were only an extension of his principal. Agency rules are important because very often when people deal with business entities they do so only through agents. For example, no one can personally do business with a corporation; one can only deal with people representing the corporation. Note that if the principal makes it appear to the public that someone is authorized as her agent, then the public has a right to rely on that person's words and actions as if they were the words and actions of the principal. For example, if a retail establishment makes it appear that its employee, Sam Wallace, is authorized to discount certain merchandise, and he does so for a certain customer, then that customer is entitled to the discount even if the retailer later says that Mr. Wallace actually was told not to discount the merchandise. According to contract and agency law, the contract is between the retailer (represented by agent Wallace) and the customer who reasonably relied on appearances of authority created by the retailer. The mix-up between the retailer and Mr. Wallace is not the concern of the customer, but rather is a matter to be resolved between Mr. Wallace and his employer.

Consumer Protection Law

In recent times, federal, state, and local laws have added many new consumer protections to basic contract law. A few of the more notable ones are described in this section. Although some of these laws create tort liability, they will be covered in this section since they address wrongful conduct associated with the making of contracts.

Many consumer protection laws at the federal level are in the form of federal agency rules and regulations. The Federal Trade Commission was created in part to prevent unfair and deceptive trade practices. To carry out this mandate the Commission has promulgated rules relating to used car sales,[30] funeral home services,[31] door-to-door sales,[32] and other transactions. Perhaps the most important of these for small claims purposes is the door-to-door sales rule. The rule permits a consumer (one who makes a purchase for his own use or consumption), who buys, rents, or leases goods or services for $25.00 or more, for cash or on credit, to withdraw from the contract within three days if it was entered into as a result of a home solicitation. If the consumer withdraws, the contract is canceled, and the consumer is entitled to the return of any money paid to the other party. Many states have a similar rule that should be researched in the event the federal rule does not apply. New York's version is contained in Personal Property Law Article 10-A.[33]

Most other federal agencies that deal with consumer protection, such as the Food and Drug Administration and Consumer Product Safety Commission, focus on such issues of national concern as maintaining a safe food supply and eliminating dangerous consumer products. Their rules and regulations would not be helpful in most small claims disputes.

State legislatures increasingly have passed consumer protection laws. In New York, many of these are found in the General Business Law[34] statute. The laws in that statute with broader application are presented below.

Section 349 declares unlawful "[d]eceptive acts or practices in the conduct of any business, trade or commerce or in the furnishing of any service in this state."[35] This section authorizes individual victims to sue in their own names[36] to recover actual losses suffered or a minimum of fifty dollars in cases where actual losses are less than that.[37] The minimum offers some incentive even in the smallest of claims. In addition, the court may grant plaintiffs a modified treble damage award; that is, an "award of damages ... not to exceed three times the actual damages up to one thousand dollars, if the court finds the defendant willfully or knowingly violated [the] section."[38] Finally, individual plaintiffs also may be awarded reasonable attorney's fees.[39] This last provision may present the biggest threat to a wrongdoing defendant given the high cost of lawyers' services in New York. Some municipalities, such as New York City, have similar laws applicable within their jurisdictions. Section 389 expressly includes as deceptive practices the manufacturing, rebuilding, and selling of "bedding in this state that contains any used material ... unless it bears a conspicuous yellow label notifying the consumer of that fact."[40]

Section 772 imposes, in addition to any compensatory damages, a "penalty of five hundred dollars plus reasonable attorney's fees" upon a contractor who induces a person to enter into a home improvement contract through false or fraudulent written statements.[41]

Section 350 declares unlawful "[f]alse advertising in the conduct of any business, trade or commerce or in the furnishing of any service in this state."[42] False advertising is that which is "misleading in a material respect."[43] False advertising is a wrong committed by the business entity; no wrong is committed by the medium through which the business advertises.[44] The New York State Attorney General is authorized to bring actions,[45] and individual victims are authorized to sue in their own names, to recover the greater of actual losses suffered or fifty dollars, enjoin the activity, or both.[46] In addition, individual plaintiffs may be granted a treble damage award up to $1,000.00 if the court finds the defendant willfully or knowingly violated the section.[47] Individual plaintiffs also may be awarded reasonable attorney's fees in the discretion of the court.[48]

Article 30[49] addresses contractual agreements between customers and a wide variety of health-related clubs and organizations. Some of the more notable provisions prohibit terms exceeding three years[50] and permit cancellation of such contracts within three business days, or whenever the consumer presents a statement from a doctor indicating the patient's inability to "receive the services because of significant physical disability for a period in excess of six months," or whenever the customer moves "more than twenty-five miles from any health club operated by seller."[51] An individual plaintiff may be awarded treble damages and reasonable attorney's fees, if her health club violates the rules in the article.[52]

Two sections of the statute include the so-called *lemon laws* for new[53] and used cars.[54] Both laws grant purchasers of vehicles the right to exchange or return them in certain circumstances. Typically, purchasers pursue their rights through an arbitration process arranged through the New York State Attorney General's office.

Section 396-u requires the seller-dealer of furniture and major household appliances[55] to provide an estimated delivery date or range, notification of any delay together with a revised delivery date, and disclosure of the customer's right either to cancel the contract with full refund or store credit at customer's option, arrange a new delivery date, or select different goods.[56] Individual plaintiffs who establish a violation by the seller may be awarded the greater of treble damages or $100, and reasonable attorney's fees.[57]

Article 35-D creates a type of *lemon law* for certain pets.[58] This article grants purchasers of dogs and cats the right to return the animal for either a full refund or another animal, or to be reimbursed for veterinary expenses if the purchaser presents within 14 business days of purchase, a licensed veterinarian's certification that the animal is "unfit for purchase" because of illness, disease, or malformation.[59] The law applies only to sales by pet dealers, as therein defined.

DAMAGES

Measure of Damages

The amount of money to which a prevailing party is entitled in a breach of contract case is the amount of foreseeable financial loss actually sustained by reason of the breach.[60] The courts seek to place the victim in the same financial position that he would have been in had the breach not occurred. Neither reward nor penalty is included in the court's judgment. Recovery is limited to foreseeable losses, meaning only those that directly and naturally result from the breach, or those that were contemplated by the parties at the time the contract was made. Consequences such as inconvenience and annoyance generally are not compensable injuries.

In some cases, one party will breach but the other will have no resulting loss. Suing almost always is pointless in such cases since a court could not award damages other than in a nominal amount, such as one dollar. For example, if a contracting buyer of a used automobile refuses to pay and take delivery of the car, he is in breach. If, however, several other buyers are lined up to pay the same amount or more money for the car, the seller has no damage because he will suffer no losses due to the buyer's actions. On the other hand, if the only other buyer on the scene was willing to pay $500.00 less than the original buyer, the seller would be suffering a loss of $500.00 recoverable from the original buyer in a breach of contract action.

Losses that may or may not occur in the future or losses that may or may not be attributable to the breach generally are not recoverable. For example, if a celebrity contracts to put her name on a magazine and otherwise support it, but then walks away from her responsibilities, the publisher cannot recover for profits lost on future sales absent persuasive evidence that there would have been such profitability in the future.[61]

Liquidated Damages/Limitation of Damages

The computation of damages in breach of contract cases may be difficult and time-consuming. Consequently, parties sometimes include in their agreements a provision, called a liquidated damages clause, stating the amount of money one party must pay the other if she breaches. Such provisions often require forfeiture of amounts previously paid, such as a deposit, in the event of breach. The courts will recognize and enforce a liquidated damages clause if at contract time it seemed that the actual amount of losses would be difficult to ascertain in the event of breach and the amount set forth in the clause was a reasonable estimate of actual losses.[62] Courts refuse to enforce clauses that do not meet these requirements since they are more in the nature of penalties for breach rather than good faith estimates of actual losses.

The parties may agree to limit the amount of damages payable if there is a breach. Limitations are common in film-developing and dry-cleaning contracts. They are enforceable unless the court finds reasons that they should be ignored.

Duty to Minimize Damages

The party suffering a loss from a breach has a duty to take reasonable steps to minimize the loss.[63] He is not free to stand idly by while the losses from another's breach mount up. For example, if a wedding photographer under contract is fired without cause six months before the wedding, he would be expected to take reasonable steps to obtain substitute work for that date. Plaintiffs who have not fulfilled this duty may fail to recover all or a portion of their alleged damages.

Chapter 4

Tort Cases

Private legal wrongs other than breaches of contract are referred to as torts. The word *tort* is derived from the French word for *twisted* and refers to behavior that has been declared unlawful. Another way of understanding torts is as wrongs committed by a person who breaches a duty to another, where that duty is created by a law rather than a contractual agreement. The distinction between breaches of contract and torts, then, lies in the source of the duty. The law creating the tort duty usually is in the form of a court decision or a statute. State courts have been very active over centuries in proscribing certain behavior in society and authorizing civil litigation for misbehavior. State legislatures have been more active participants in recent times.

The three types of torts are intentional torts, negligence, and strict liability torts. Intentional torts comprise a wide range of deliberate acts. Negligence is unintentional, yet wrongful behavior. Finally, the strict liability torts involve behavior that may not be improper, yet is considered unlawful. In the next section, general tort principles and specific examples of the various types of torts will be discussed.

Certain behavior simultaneously constitutes both a tort and a crime. For example, a person who has committed the tort of *conversion* against an automobile owner by stealing her car, has engaged in behavior that also constitutes the crime of *larceny*. In such a case, the wrongdoer may be tried by the state for his crime and also separately sued by his individual victim for money damages. Generally, the criminal proceeding would occur first, followed by the civil case against the wrongdoer. The two proceedings would be held before different judges with different procedural rules, and in rare cases, result in different outcomes. The foremost example of this dualism is the pair of famous California cases involving O.J. Simpson and the deaths of Nicole Simpson and Ronald Goldman. In the criminal trial of Mr. Simpson the jury rendered a "not guilty" of murder verdict.[64] The families of the victims sued Mr. Simpson for various torts associated with wrongfully causing the deaths of their loved ones. In the civil case tried according to different procedures before a different judge, a different jury rendered a verdict holding Mr. Simpson liable for the two deaths and awarded money damages to the plaintiffs. The decision was affirmed on appeal.[65] Of course, if a person is found guilty after a criminal trial, she would almost certainly be found liable in a subsequent civil trial involving the same behavior, since less evidence is needed to win a civil case than a criminal case. This chapter deals only with civil law and liability.

LIABILITY

The three classes of torts are intentional, negligence, and strict liability. The first class consists of many torts each of which addresses specific deliberate behavior such as striking another person, stealing another's property, and damaging another's reputation through lies. Each intentional tort bears a unique name; the wrongful acts described above are the torts of *battery*, *conversion*, and *defamation*. The second category consists of the single tort of negligence, which may be committed in innumerable ways. Negligence is the most complicated of torts to explain and the most commonly litigated. The final group is a small one that originally included a few lawful activities considered to be so dangerous that anyone who engaged in them had to bear all the inherent risk. Examples of activities that give rise to strict liability include the keeping of wild animals and blasting with explosives. In recent times, the courts in most states also have imposed strict liability on merchant-sellers for personal injuries caused by their defective merchandise. A person who causes harm by conducting any of these activities is strictly or absolutely liable to the victim, meaning liable whether or not the accused did anything improper in the conduct of the activity. These torts so rarely are litigated in small claims court that they are not covered further in this book.

Intentional Torts – General

Each intentional tort is well defined in the law wherein the associated legal duty is created. Most often these torts are established in case law. Typically, the duty and the tort are established as a result of one person suing another for allegedly wrongful behavior. When the court that is entertaining the action determines that the behavior is not only wrongful but also should be made illegal, it recognizes a new legal responsibility to avoid the behavior and concomitant right to sue for breach of that duty. Over time, more persons sue for alleged commission of the tort against them. In their cases the courts refine the definition and applicability of the tort as necessary. Taken together, all the court cases addressing the tort give us the law for that tort. Consequently, researching these torts is interesting but difficult. Definitions and examples of some of the intentional torts litigated in small claims court are included in this chapter. To establish liability in an intentional tort case, a claimant must look to the definition of the tort and submit evidence to establish each element of the cause of action derived from the definition. Generally, this means showing which law prohibits the defendant's alleged behavior, proving the defendant engaged in the behavior, and proving that the wrongful behavior resulted in damage to the plaintiff.

The consumer-related intentional torts of false advertising and deceptive trade practices were discussed in Chapter Three. A third related tort called fraud is addressed below. Following that, battery and trespass to personal property are treated.

Intentional Torts – Fraud

The tort of fraud is committed by a person who, in the course of a transaction, intentionally misrepresents or actively conceals a material fact upon which her victim justifiably relies to his detriment.[66] Often the most difficult part of a fraud case is proving the defendant's intent since defendants usually claim they did not lie but were simply unaware of the real facts. A claimant must establish, in effect, that the defendant deliberately deceived him about a factual matter and the claimant had no reasonable way to see through the deceit. In transactions between strangers, there is no absolute legal right to trust the other person. Each person must take reasonable precautions to assure that the other is being truthful.

Sometimes even a failure to voluntarily speak up about important facts is fraudulent. If, in the course of a transaction, a person who knows relevant, undiscoverable facts involving health and safety dangers deliberately refrains from volunteering the information, he may be found liable for fraud. In a case in Nassau County, New York, a house seller did not disclose information about a pesticide spill at the house.[67] After purchasing the house and living in it for some time, the buyers learned that the house was contaminated with the carcinogenic pesticide chlordane and sued the seller for committing fraud by deliberately withholding the information. If the seller did not know of the problem, she did not commit fraud. The buyers had to prove she knew and deliberately held back the information. They did so by way of evidence that she disclosed the problem to someone else before the house sale. Although the buyers won a substantial amount of money in what clearly was not a small claims case, the same principles apply.

If the victim of fraud seeks money damages in court she must prove the extent of the harm suffered. Alternatively, the fraud victim may seek an undoing of the contract, called rescission, as her remedy. In that case the parties simply would be put back in the positions they were in before the contract was made, without the award of any additional money damages. Although rescission is not a remedy available in small claims court, an award of money, conditioned on the return of property to the other party, is permitted.

Intentional Torts – Battery

The wrongful act that constitutes battery is the intentional, harmful or offensive physical contact with another person in other than a lawful context.[68] When one person intentionally interferes with another's personal dignity through physical contact he runs the risk of being sued for battery. This tort may be committed even if the behavior does not constitute a criminal assault; tort law prohibits even offensive contact. Examples of battery include the following deliberate behaviors: striking someone with fists or feet (but not if sanctioned in a sporting event), rape, shooting someone with a gun, hitting a person with a rock or other object, blowing tobacco smoke in someone's face, and uninvited intimate touching of another person. Evidence is needed to establish all parts of the definition, and in many cases, to refute the defense of self-defense. Eyewitness testimony or a police report, or both, may be necessary to prove a battery case.

In the cases of harmful contact, the amount of damages awarded will reflect the severity of physical injury; for offensive contact, damages are predicated on humiliation and other factors.

Intentional Torts – Trespass to Personal Property

The tort of trespass to personal property is committed when one person intentionally damages the personal property of another person or otherwise interferes with it.[69] Personal property includes virtually everything a person owns other than land and buildings. Defacing someone's artwork, deliberately scratching a person's car, or breaking the windshield are examples of this tort. The most difficult part of these cases to prove is the identity of the wrongdoer. Often a claimant will have suspicions but will be unable to prove them in court.

Negligence – General

Negligence is the most litigated tort. The wrongful behavior that underlies the cause of action is committed without intent (it often is described as *accidental*), and may be described generally as the failure to execute any legal duty that causes direct or reasonably foreseeable harm to another person or property. The essence of the wrong is not in bad intent but in a failure to live up to applicable standards imposed by law. Negligence law creates certain minimum standards of care that must be observed between people with respect to many activities. Some of these standards are set forth in statutes, such as the traffic laws, and others are contained in case law. Liability is established by showing which legal duty the defendant owed, how he breached it, and how that breach caused the claimant's problem. No effort is made here to list all legal duties that could give rise to negligence claims. Instead, those that are more likely to be the subject of negligence claims in small claims court are discussed in general terms. They are the duties of automobile drivers, pet owners, bailees, and landowners.

Negligence – Automobile Drivers

In New York, most legal obligations of automobile drivers are contained in the statute known as the Vehicle and Traffic Law.[70] Violations of traffic laws almost always are considered breaches of legal duty for negligence purposes, and if harm or damage is thereby caused, negligence is committed. For example, if a driver passes a stop sign without stopping and no damage is done, she is subject only to the "public" punishment of a fine. If, however, in passing the stop sign she causes a collision, she will face public punishment, *and* the victim will be permitted to recover money damages because the driver breached a legal duty owed to the victim, thereby causing harm. In presenting negligent driving cases in court, liability of the defendant often is partially established through a police report, eyewitnesses, and photographs showing the type and placement of damage to each car. Diagrams often are helpful. Courts may divide fault in negligence cases, so a claimant who is partially at fault will not receive a full recovery, and if countersued, will have to pay for part of the defendant's damage. The duties of drivers are too numerous to mention here, but the Vehicle and Traffic Law index discloses most of them.

Negligence – Pet Owners

Pet owners sometimes are sued when their pets allegedly cause injury to other persons or animals. New York law holds a dog owner liable for injuries caused by his vicious dog if he has knowledge of the dog's propensities.[71] Conversely, if the owner has no reason to believe his pet is vicious, he is not liable for injuries inflicted by the animal unless the owner's lack of ordinary care caused the incident. This sometimes is referred to as the "one free bite" rule, because until after such time as a pet bites another animal or person, the owner of an otherwise normal pet usually has no reason to believe the pet dangerous and has no liability absent negligence on his part. Obviously, the critical evidence in such a case will relate to the owner's knowledge of his pet's propensities. Separately, there is a duty established in the ordinances of most municipalities to keep dogs within the confines of the owner's property, or if off-premises, on a leash. Failure to do so may be held a breach of duty supporting a negligence claim for property damage caused by the unattended animal.

Negligence – Bailees

Bailees are persons or companies to whom others, called bailors, deliver temporary possession of an item or items of personal property pursuant to an agreement.[72] The delivery may be for storage, transport, to have work done on the property, or other reasons. The relationship between the bailor and the bailee is called a bailment. Leaving clothes with a dry-cleaner, leaving a car to be valet-parked, and renting an automobile are common examples of bailments. According to case law, bailees who receive any form of compensation owe a duty to use ordinary care with the owner's property during the term of the bailment.[73] In no-compensation situations, bailees will owe a duty to use more or less care depending upon which party is benefitting from the bailment. Failure to exercise the required level of care is a breach of legal duty. If the breach causes damage or loss, the bailee has committed negligence and is liable to the owner. If, however, a loss occurs through no fault of the bailee, there is no negligence, and the bailee is not liable. Separately, if the bailee delivers the property to the wrong person causing a loss to the owner, the bailee is liable for that loss even in the absence of negligence.

When alleging negligence, plaintiff-bailors who establish a bailment context benefit from the *presumption of negligence* rule. The court-made rule works this way: once a claimant alleging negligence by a bailee establishes in court that the defendant accepted the property agreeing to act as a bailee and that the property is lost or damaged, negligence by the defendant is presumed. The defendant is given a chance to produce evidence showing that the loss or damage was caused by reasons other than his negligence. If the defendant is unable to do so, the claimant wins the case. The rule relieves the claimant of the usual burden of producing evidence showing exactly how the defendant breached his duty of care and how this caused the loss or damage. The defendant-bailee, therefore, has the greater burden in bailment-related negligence cases. The claimant's evidence of the bailment relationship with the defendant typically is a written agreement between them or testimony accompanied by some written evidence, such as a receipt from the defendant for the property in question. The bailment agreement must be reviewed as part of the determination of liability and damages in any bailment case. By their agreement, a bailor and bailee may substitute some rules of their own choosing for the ordinary bailment rules. For example, they may agree to a limitation of liability. Most agreed-upon provisions are

enforceable in court; some are not. An example of an unen-
forceable provision is a disclaimer of liability for damages due
to negligence by automobile parking lots and garages with
spaces for four or more vehicles.[74]

In cases where the bailee is accused of damaging the property, the condition of the property when bailed often becomes
an issue. The defendant may claim that the alleged damage
pre-existed the bailment. That dispute may come down to a
credibility issue, meaning the judge or arbitrator looks
carefully for evidence as to which party is more believable. To
avoid this problem, include in the bailment agreement a note
about pre-existing damage or the lack of it. For example,
when renting a car it is wise for the renter to include in the
written agreement a note about any pre-existing dents,
scratches, and the like, so as not to be held responsible for
them later.

Negligence – Landowners

Commercial and residential property owners have a legal
duty to persons that they have reason to know or believe will
be on the property to keep them reasonably safe from harm
caused by defects in the property.[75] Failure to repair or
remove trip hazards on the ground, failure to properly clear
sidewalks of ice or snow, failure to warn of a wet or slippery
floor, poor lighting, and any number of other forms of potentially dangerous activity, or inactivity, may be breaches of
duty. Many claims of this type are processed through property
insurers without recourse to court. If no settlement is reached,
however, court action is appropriate. Attorneys representing
persons alleging serious physical injury bring such claims in
higher-level courts since large recoveries are anticipated.

The identity of the party responsible to execute the legal
duty with respect to the property must be determined in these
cases. For example, for leased property, the responsible party
may be the landlord or the tenant; for a sidewalk, the
municipality or adjacent property owner. Claimants who are

unsure about responsibility often sue all potentially responsible parties and resolve the issue in court.

Other Law Affecting Liability

Agency Law

Review the treatment of agency law in Chapter Three. Related concepts are addressed here.

Negligence law is significantly affected by the rule of *respondeat superior*. The rule imposes **vicarious** liability on employers for torts committed by employees within the scope of employment.[76] The liability is called *vicarious* because the employer herself has done nothing wrong or illegal but is held responsible solely because of her relationship to the wrong-doer. According to the court-made rule, since the employee is acting for the employer at her direction and is furthering her interests, the employer should answer for torts associated with that conduct. *Respondeat superior* often is invoked in negligence cases; however, it may be applied in intentional tort cases if it is shown that the employee committing the intentional tort did so in furtherance of his employer's interests, rather than as a purely personal matter. For example, a bar bouncer who intentionally strikes a patron may himself be liable for the intentional tort of battery, and *respondeat superior* may be invoked if the act was related to his employment.

Because of this rule, employers often are sued along with their employees when torts by the employees are alleged. Typically, the employer will be in a better financial position to pay any resulting judgment. Persons or companies, sued as alleged employers under the rule, often defend by claiming either that they are not the accused person's employer, or the person was not acting within the scope of employment when he committed the alleged wrong.

Some hallmarks of an employer-employee relationship are a long-term work relationship, the right to direct, control, and supervise the worker's acts, and the payment to the worker of regular compensation rather than a lump sum. If a worker is not an employee, he may be an independent contractor, such as a home improvement contractor, who hires himself out to others by way of individual contracts. Employers of independent contractors generally are not subject to the *respondeat superior* rule.

Acting within the scope of employment generally means acting in furtherance of the employer's interests. Making deliveries for the employer, carrying out employment duties during work hours, conducting sales calls, and attending work-related seminars are some activities considered to be in the scope of employment. Employees are not acting within the scope of employment when they are pursuing purely personal interests of their own. For most people, commuting to and from the place of employment and conducting personal errands on lunch break, are outside the scope. Similarly, any other activities completely unrelated to the employer's business or interests are outside the scope.

A second and very important example of vicarious liability in New York State is an automobile owner's liability for the negligent driving of any person using the automobile with the owner's permission.[77] The rule is important to remember both for owners who might give such permission and victims of negligent drivers.

DAMAGES

Compensatory Damages

In tort cases, the goal of the monetary damages award is to compensate the claimant for harm done by making the claimant whole through the payment of money to her.[78] Personal injury and property damage are compensable. If a claimant has suffered physical injury and has established liability against the defendant, she is entitled to an amount of money necessary to compensate her for proved financial losses, such as medical expenses incurred, lost wages, and future medical expenses. She also is entitled to money for past and projected pain and suffering, psychological injury, and loss of enjoyment of life. These are more subjective and require a careful evaluation of testimony and other evidence. Pain and suffering awards sometimes are determined as a multiple, such as two or three times, of out-of-pocket losses. Such damages calculations are not often made in small claims court because if a claimant has suffered significant pain and suffering, his case probably will be handled by an attorney in a higher-level court where the recovery is unlimited. Nevertheless, to avoid underestimating the value of the claim, anyone filing such a claim in small claims court is well advised to seek the maximum money recoverable in the court when filing the statement of claim. Evidence might include physicians' bills, hospital records, a physician's affidavit or testimony, pharmacy bills, and the claimant's testimony.

If property damage or loss is claimed, one of several measures is used to determine the amount of compensatory damages. If property is damaged, the measure usually is the difference between the property's market value immediately before and immediately after it was damaged, or the reasonable cost of repairs necessary to restore it to its former condition, whichever is less.[79] In certain cases, however, such as loss of ,or significant damage to clothing, this measure is inappropriate because the property cannot be repaired and does not have a market value that reflects its value to the owner. In these cases, courts generally will grant as damages, the unique value to the owner or the amount of the purchase price less an amount for depreciation, whichever is more appropriate in the circumstances. For example, in a case where a film developing service negligently loses a customer's photographs, the measure of damages will be the unique value of those photographs to the customer, since the photographs have no market value or purchase price. The damages recoverable in such a case, however, may be limited by a clause in the contract. Evidence in property damage cases may include bill of sale or receipt for purchase, itemized paid bill for repairs made, two itemized estimates for repairs needed, photographs of the property, the property itself when feasible, and testimony of unique value, if appropriate.

Punitive Damages

An additional award of money to the claimant, called punitive damages, is available in intentional tort and gross negligence cases but not in ordinary negligence cases.[80] Punitive damages are awarded when deemed necessary to send a strong message that the wrongful behavior is intolerable. In non-jury trials, the judge determines the amount based in part on the defendant's overall financial resources and ability to pay. In order to make the option of punitive damages available in an appropriate case, the claimant should request them in the small claims statement of claim. Evidence may include testimony, photographs, medical reports, and the like, showing the egregiousness of the defendant's acts and extent of injuries suffered, and financial records or public records showing the defendant's financial resources. Punitive damages may not be imposed against municipalities.[81]

Chapter 5

Researching the Law

The major primary sources of contract and tort law are state court decisions and state statutes. New York's statutes are published in books and electronic media. Printed statutes may be found for example, in publications by Looseleaf Law Publications, Inc., *McKinney's Consolidated Laws of New York Annotated* and *Consolidated Laws Service*. One or more are available at many public and courthouse libraries and the statutes may be viewed on certain Web sites. Statutes are organized by topic in alphabetically arranged titles with individual indices and a general index. For example, most traffic laws are contained in the *Vehicle and Traffic Law* title, and many laws relating to alcohol are found in the *Alcoholic Beverage Control Law* title. Sometimes, however, the contents of the title are not so clearly reflected in the name of the title. A researcher might peruse the volumes to determine where to start looking for certain statutory law or refer to the general index at the end of the set of books.

New York State court decisions are published in books called reporters. Court of Appeals (New York's highest court) decisions are published in *New York Reports*. Appellate Division (New York's middle level court) decisions are published in *Appellate Division Reports*. Other (trial level) court decisions are published in *Miscellaneous Reports*. Many decisions of the aforementioned courts also are published in another set of books called *New York Supplement*. Although these books may be available in law school, courthouse, and the larger public libraries, they rarely are available at smaller public libraries. Researching case law is extremely difficult. Cases are arranged in the reporters roughly in chronological sequence without regard to the subject matter of the cases. A researcher must refer to other books, called digests, to determine which cases are relevant to her research and in which volumes of reporters they are published. Digests are arranged by legal topic and show the names and citations of court cases relevant to those topics. Citations are the numbers and abbreviations by which case decisions are located within the reporters. The key to using the digests for legal research is in knowing the subject matter topic under which to look for case decisions. Non-lawyers are at a tremendous disadvantage because the subject titles often are technical terms that only lawyers fully understand.

Reading and understanding judicial opinions is challenging, especially if the legal topic is complex. Researchers must be aware of the additional problem of determining if the legal ruling in any particular case has been modified or overruled by a later decision in another case or even the same case. Laymen conducting research should be very careful not to imagine that they have become more knowledgeable about the law relating to their cases than the judges or arbitrators to whom they will present those cases. The major benefit of legal research for the small claims litigant is to help her analyze the relative strength of her case and to guide her in the preparation of her evidence.

For the stated reasons, and others, the easier road for a litigant determined to conduct legal research is to use sources that summarize or explain the law. One may use the services of an attorney in this manner. Rather than incur the expense of engaging an attorney for the litigation, a claimant may arrange a brief consultation for guidance in handling her own claim. Depending on the value of the claim, this may be a very efficient way of preparing for trial.

A well respected source that is relied upon by lawyers and judges in New York State is the legal encyclopedia called *New York Jurisprudence*. Although it is intended for lawyers, the encyclopedia may be useful to others since it condenses a vast amount of New York statutory and case law in one set of books organized by topic. As with case digests, the key to successfully using *New York Jurisprudence* is in knowing which topic to review to find the treatment of relevant law. A non-lawyer may spend many hours before discovering the right topic for his case, and if the material is indexed under a technical term or phrase whose meaning is not known to the researcher, he will be unable to find it. For much simpler and briefer explanations of New York law for laymen, New York State Bar Association publications may be consulted. Visit the Association's Web site at www.nysba.org. Some of the aforementioned sources are available free of charge via the Internet at Web sites such as www.law.cornell. edu and www.findlaw.com. Numerous governmental Web sites are filled with useful law-related information. Some of these are identified in Chapter Six. Of course, commercial online legal research services such as Westlaw® and Lexis® include extensive databases of laws and related information, but are not readily available to the general public. Many state laws are available for your personal computer or hand held device through www.looseleaflaw.com.

Chapter 6

Alternatives to Court

Several alternatives are available to persons whose disputes are not appropriate for small claims court or who are willing to try other approaches before resorting to litigation. A person who believes he has a valid claim against another may attempt to negotiate a resolution directly, seek assistance from a private dispute resolution organization, or utilize the services of a government office or agency.

PERSONAL NEGOTIATION

Trying to resolve a problem through personal negotiation is a natural first response in many instances. Following a fender-bender, people often agree to acquire estimates and make appropriate payments. A purchaser of defective merchandise may return to the merchant, request a refund of the purchase price, and receive it. Sometimes more negotiation is required, but generally it is worth the effort for several reasons. First, the process may be easier than imagined, especially if all parties behave rationally. Second, there is nothing to lose by attempting settlement. Other forms of resolution remain available should settlement not be reached. Third, parties who agree to pay as a result of settlement negotiations statistically are more likely to pay than those who lose a court case. Finally, the parties will save time and reduce inconvenience by avoiding litigation.

Negotiation typically begins informally with oral communication. Sometimes nothing more is needed to reach agreement. If, however, a quick informal settlement is not reached, a person seeking settlement is well advised to reduce her version of the problem to a typed letter that is short and polite and to send it to the other person by certified mail, return receipt requested. The letter should clearly indicate that if the recipient does not respond by a stated deadline, the sender will resort to other methods of resolution, including litigation. As with all important documents, the sender should keep a copy of the letter.

Some people are better than others when it comes to negotiating; however, everyone can be successful if a few important guidelines are followed. Remaining calm and polite, yet firm, expresses confidence. Showing some knowledge of the relevant law exhibits competence and seriousness. Finally, deciding the exact amount of money that is acceptable for settlement, in advance of serious settlement talks, eliminates hesitance and increases the chance that a deal will be struck. If the parties reach agreement to resolve the problem by some future action, such as the payment of money, one of them should quickly put it in writing and both parties should sign it. This discourages a denial of the settlement. Once the agreement is included in a signed writing, it becomes a written contract fully enforceable in court as such, without any need to prove the facts relating to the underlying dispute. For example, if the parties in a fender-bender sign a written settlement agreement whereby Wilson agrees to pay Alvarez $500.00, that contract is enforceable against Wilson if he breaches by failing to pay, without any need for evidence of who caused the fender-bender.

If one does not wish to personally negotiate a settlement, it always is appropriate to utilize the services of a professional, such as an attorney, to do so on one's behalf.

PRIVATE ORGANIZATIONS AND MEDIATION

Many private organizations will assist individuals seeking negotiated settlements. Perhaps the best known is the Better Business Bureau. At its Web site, www.bbb.org, the organization states, "We will work with you and the business to reach a solution to your problem." The process by which a third party, such as the Better Business Bureau, assists disputants in discussing their differences and reaching a mutually satisfactory settlement is called **mediation**. The third party, called a mediator, helps them focus on the factual issues rather than the emotional or personal aspects of the problem. Mediation works best when the parties have a good faith dispute and neither party is completely in the wrong. The mediator seeks to bring both sides together, move them away from hardened positions, and find common ground where each party concedes a little in the interests of resolving the problem. The Better Business Bureau also offers conciliation and arbitration services.

In New York, mediation also is conducted at Community Dispute Resolution Centers throughout the state. The Centers, established pursuant to Article 21-A of New York's Judiciary Law,[82] offer an alternative approach to solving problems that develop between people. Instead of resorting to criminal or civil court, the disputants sit down with a trained neutral mediator and try to work out a mutually agreeable solution to their problem. The Centers fulfill several valuable purposes. First, they provide a place and program to work out problems. Second, they help prevent the escalation of disputes to more serious civil or criminal matters. Third, they relieve the court system of a number of matters that do not require the formal structure and process of a courtroom. Finally, they provide an educational experience in peaceful problem-solving.

The Centers are private, non-profit community-based agencies that contract to provide dispute resolution services to citizens and the justice system. Anyone may make referrals to the Centers, including family members, friends, neighbors, clergy, schools, law enforcement agencies, lawyers, employers, public and private agencies, district attorneys, and judges. A directory of Community Dispute Resolution Centers may be accessed via the World Wide Web at www.nysdra.org by clicking on the "Find a CDRC" button.

Mediations at the Centers proceed as follows. Initially, the person seeking mediation contacts the local office. A staff member schedules an appointment for the disputants. The mediation process may be conducted by one or two volunteer mediators. Mediators must be neutral, so any association between mediator and disputant disqualifies the mediator. As the parties sit around a table, the mediator begins the process by introducing himself and explaining how the mediation will be conducted. The steps include: listening, clarifying, asking questions, understanding, and encouraging exchange and agreement. The mediators help the disputants by letting them talk out the problem in a neutral environment. No record is made of the proceeding. Each disputant may meet privately with the mediator, if necessary.

Typical disputes brought to Mediation Centers include both private and public matters, such as assault and harassment cases, problems relating to pets, breach of contract, consumer/merchant disputes, criminal trespass, employer/employee issues, family matters, forgery, bad check, landlord/tenant, menacing, neighbor problems, theft of services, violation of ordinances, and some felonies.

Media organizations can assist in dispute resolution. If a consumer encounters an unresolved problem with a product or service, she may obtain satisfaction by contacting media outlets in which the product or service has been advertised. Newspapers, magazines, and the like do not want to advertise products or services that may by implication damage their reputations or involve them in litigation. They may pressure the seller to settle. Checking with the local newspapers and television stations to see if they have a "Consumer Action Line," "Action Reporter," or similarly titled feature also may be helpful. Adverse publicity is a powerful incentive to settle a dispute.

PUBLIC AGENCIES

Offices of government officials, such as the governor, county executives, and mayors, may include divisions offering dispute resolution assistance. Through its Bureau of Consumer Frauds and Protection, the New York State Attorney General's Office acts for consumers at no cost when misleading or unlawful business practices are alleged. Automobile Lemon Law disputes also are handled through the Attorney General's Office. Readers are referred to the Attorney General's Web site, www.ag.ny.gov, for more information. Check your local government offices for similar departments.

Various administrative agencies of government offer assistance to parties with disputes relating to their area of authority. For example, in New York City persons with disputes relating to rental property might obtain assistance from the New York City Rent Guidelines Board at www.housingnyc.com and persons with automotive repair complaints may be assisted by the New York State Department of Motor Vehicles, Division of Vehicle Safety at www.nydmv.state.ny.us.

Finally, various agencies of government at the federal, state, and local levels are dedicated exclusively to consumer protection. Information from the federal government is found at www.usa.gov/Citizen/Topics/Consumer_Safety.shtml. New York State has a Consumer Protection Board proclaimed to be "the State's top consumer watchdog," with a Web site at www.consumer.state.ny.us featuring "consumer links" and a "consumer law help manual." New York City has its Department of Consumer Affairs, with a Web address at www.ci.nyc.ny.us/html/dca/html/home/home.shtml. Other cities and counties have similar agencies, such as the Nassau County Office of Consumer Affairs that may be consulted at www.nassaucountyny.gov/agencies/oca/index.html.

Chapter 7

Small Claims Actions

I n this chapter procedural and substantive law issues relevant to small claims and powers of the courts adjudicating small claims in New York State are presented. A step-by-step description of the process of litigating a small claim with practical advice completes the chapter.

THE COURT

Powers and Limitations

Small claims are heard in several courts throughout New York State; however, none of the courts is officially entitled as "Small Claims Court." The claims are heard in the small claims *parts* of lower-level trial courts that also adjudicate other types of cases. Nevertheless, for the sake of simplicity I refer to those parts as *small claims court* throughout this book. Although the parts were specifically created to handle small claims, persons with such claims are not precluded from suing in the regular part of the court with attorneys and application of all the strict rules of civil procedure.[83] Small claims court, however, is by far the more popular place to bring such claims.

In New York City, small claims parts are found in New York City Civil Court. In other cities in the state, they are in City Courts. In Nassau County and parts of Suffolk County on Long Island, District Courts have small claims parts. In all other locations they may be found in Justice Courts, which are identified as Town or Village Courts. The four distinct governing statutory articles for these small claims parts are found in New York's Judiciary Law – Court Acts[84] and are reprinted as separate appendices to this book. Each is identified as Article 18 of its relevant court act – New York City Civil Court Act for New York City Civil Court, Uniform City Court Act for City Courts, Uniform District Court Act for District Courts and Uniform Justice Court Act for Town and

Village Courts. Although there are some differences, the articles are in large part identical in content. The sources for the following discussion of small claims court are Article 18 of the New York City Civil Court Act ("Court Act" in this book), reprinted as Appendix A hereto, and the relevant part of the Uniform Civil Rules for the New York City Civil Court ("Uniform Rules" in this book) established thereunder, also reprinted as an appendix. Users of the other courts should consult the appropriate statutory law and related rules. Finally, the New York statute known as Civil Practice Law and Rules, the primary source for general civil procedural law, also governs small claims to the extent it is not inconsistent with the small claims statute. Some important sections of the statute are reprinted as an appendix. In practice, reference to this statute is rare in small claims actions.

The maximum sum of money recoverable in small claims court is $5,000.00[85] (or $3,000.00 in the Justice Courts[86]), to which may be added an additional amount covering interest and costs of the proceeding. The $5,000.00 limit represents an increase of $2,000.00 over the previous maximum and opens the process to many more claims that would otherwise have required the services of an attorney. The limit is included within the statutory definition of *small claim*, which describes that term in part to be "any cause of action for money only not in excess of five thousand dollars exclusive of interest and costs."[87] Interest refers to an additional amount of money calculated at a rate fixed by law to which a prevailing party is entitled in certain cases. A claimant should always ask for interest in the statement of claim and at the hearing; the court will determine whether the law permits its inclusion in the judgment. The terms *hearing* and *trial* are used interchangeably in this chapter. In personal injury cases, interest begins to accrue only after the judgment date. For most other cases, interest begins to accrue upon the later of the date when plaintiff's interests were harmed or she first had the right to sue. Costs typically include filing fees paid in connection with the case. A claimant should always ask for costs in the statement of claim and at the hearing; the court will determine the issue. Since the law treats small commercial claims somewhat differently from other small claims, they will be discussed separately in this chapter.

Litigants may use small claims court for virtually any type of civil claim as long as they seek only money not exceeding the maximum. One type of money judgment that small claims court is not empowered to grant, however, relates to family law. A person seeking arrears in child support or maintenance payments may not sue in small claims court if the order granting support or maintenance is part of a New York Family Court or Supreme Court decision. Recourse is limited to those two courts.[88] A second type of money claim to be heard in a different court is a claim against the State of New York, which may be brought only in the Court of Claims.[89]

The definition of small claim clearly indicates that in an ordinary case money is the only remedy available in small claims court. Prospective litigants are urged to remember this limitation on the court's power. Neither judge nor arbitrator may grant remedies such as ordering an apology or a retraction, the return of an item, the completion of a contract, or ordering someone to stay away from the claimant. Although small claims court judges and arbitrators cannot order the transfer of property, they are authorized to condition a money judgment on "such terms as the court shall deem proper."[90] This authority may be used in various ways, including ordering the seller of defective merchandise to pay money on condition that the buyer returns the merchandise to the seller.

If a case or counterclaim potentially is worth more than the court may lawfully award, the claimant or defendant, as the case may be, may institute an action in higher level court for the full amount or bring the claim or counterclaim in small claims court and forego the amount that exceeds the permitted maximum.[91] The party must balance the potential for additional winnings with the cost of hiring an attorney familiar with practice in the higher-level court. To estimate potential winnings, review the treatment of damages in earlier chapters of this book. If a person has more than one complaint or cause of action against a defendant, and they arise out of distinct events, she may bring two or more separate actions in small claims court even if together they exceed the monetary limit.[92] If the total of all such claims does not exceed the limit, the claimant may bring one claim or separate claims.[93] If, however, the claims all arise out of the same event or transaction, they may only be brought as a single claim not to exceed the court's limit.

A small claims court's power is limited by the statutory definition of *small claim* in yet another way. The emphasized part of the definition from the Court Act shows the limitation: "The term 'small claim' or 'small claims' as used in this act shall mean and include any cause of action for money only, not in excess of five thousand dollars exclusive of interest and costs... *provided that the defendant either resides, or has an office for the transaction of business or a regular employment, within the city of New York.*"[94] A claimant is not permitted to initiate an action against any defendant who does not have one of the stated connections with the court's locale because the court would not be authorized to entertain the action. The law imposes no requirement that the claimant have a connection to the place where she sues. If, however, both the claimant and defendant are in New York City, the claim may be filed in either the claimant's or defendant's county. The small claims courts outside New York City are all similarly limited. Consequently, a claimant may only sue a defendant in the jurisdiction where the defendant lives or works even if that means seriously inconveniencing herself. Because of the relatively small amount of money at stake, this jurisdictional rule may dissuade many claimants from using small claims court when the defendant has no local connections. This type of difficulty is not of similar concern in higher-level court proceedings because the jurisdiction and venue rules are different, there is more at stake to offset any inconvenience, and the plaintiff suffers less inconvenience because of legal representation.

The aforementioned rule was determinative in *Wessell v. Porter*,[95] where a claimant tried to sue Nevison and her associate, Porter, in Erie County, New York urging the following justification for choosing that locale. Porter and Nevison leased to the claimant certain real property that they owned. The claimant sent the required rental payments to Porter's residence in Erie County, and tax bills for the leased premises also were sent there.

Nevison, who resided in California, objected to being sued in Erie County. The Buffalo City Court held that it did not have small claims jurisdiction over the case against Nevison because she did not live in the county, had no regular employment in the county, and Porter's residence in the county did not become Nevison's office for the transaction of business simply because rental payments and tax bills were sent there. Separately, the court ruled that Nevison's ownership of real property in the county did not suffice to give the court authority over the case against her.

Use of small claims court to harass others is prohibited.[96] Consequently, persons who file frivolous suits or repeat suits on the same claim may be compelled by the court or its clerk to seek permission of the court before filing a new small claim, which permission may be denied.[97]

Corporations, as well as individuals, may be sued in small claims court, provided the requisite connection to the location of the court is established.[98] Corporate defendants must be represented in court by an attorney, officer, director, or employee.[99] By her appearance in court, a non-attorney representative is deemed to have requisite authority to settle or try the case on behalf of the corporate defendant.[100] The Court Act also contemplates actions against partnerships and firms, which should include the increasingly popular limited liability companies and limited liability partnerships.

A defendant may be sued under any name in which he is conducting business, even if that is not his true name.[101] The true name of an individual is her legal name; for a partnership, firm or corporation it is the name under which it is licensed, registered, incorporated, or otherwise authorized to do business.[102] Many businesses use a trade name rather than true name in conducting business because it is catchier

or easier for people to remember. Any correction to a
defendant's name may be made before the hearing date[103] or,
is made at the latest, during the hearing on the merits.[104] A
defendant that is sued in any name in which it does business
(e.g., name on sign at premises, on vehicles, advertisements,
contracts, letterhead, invoice) is not excused from paying a
judgment simply because it is identified in the judgment by
that name rather than its true name.[105] This rule seems to be
aimed primarily at default judgments since the judge or
arbitrator must determine the true name during any hearing
at which the business defendant appears. A default judgment
is one that is entered against a defendant who fails to appear
in court on the trial date.

Partnerships, most corporations, associations, **assignees**,
and insurers are prohibited from instituting actions under the
Court Act.[106] The law is different only in District Court small
claims parts where partnerships and associations are
permitted to sue. All of these entities are permitted to sue,
however, in the separate commercial claims parts discussed
below. A corporate defendant may interpose a counterclaim as
long as it relates to the claim and the monetary and other
jurisdictional requirements are met.[107] The same rule should
apply to other legal entities.

Commercial Claims

Corporations, partnerships, and associations with their
principal offices in New York State, and their assignees, are
permitted to sue in the separate commercial claims parts
established by amendments to the New York City Civil Court
Act,[108] Uniform District Court Act,[109] and Uniform City Court
Act.[110] No such part was established for the Justice Courts.
Commercial claims are for money only subject to the same
maximum that applies in regular small claims court, and they
may only be brought against defendants who reside, have an
office for the transaction of business, or are regularly employed in the city, district, or county, as the case may be,
where the court is located. Commercial claims cases are

segregated from other small claims cases. A claimant may not bring more than five commercial claims per month. The filing fee per claim is $25.00, plus the cost of postage. Collection agencies are prohibited from using the commercial claims parts. A special demand letter must be mailed within a prescribed time period to a prospective defendant before commencing a commercial claim if it is based on a consumer transaction, defined as "a transaction between a claimant and a natural person, wherein the money, property or service which is the subject of the transaction is primarily for personal, family or household purposes."[111] Most of the other laws regulating commercial claims are identical to those regulating ordinary small claims. The governing statute for commercial claims in New York City Civil Court is reprinted as an appendix to this book.

Filing the Claim; Counterclaims, Third-party Claims and Cross-claims

A person initiates a small claims action by completing and submitting, in person or by a representative, a simple statement of claim form (see appendix) provided by the clerk at an appropriate court and paying to the clerk the correct filing fee.[112] Each court designs its own version of the form. Some courts permit claimants to submit the form by mail. Persons under 18 years of age may bring claims through a parent or legal guardian who signs the statement of claim and appears in court.[113] For claims of up to $1,000.00 the fee is $15.00; for claims over $1,000.00, the fee is $20.00.[114] The fees may be waived if the claimant appropriately establishes indigence.[115] An exception to this fee schedule is made for an employee claiming up to $300.00 in unpaid wages who must pay only the clerk's cost of mailing.[116] Of course, the fees are subject to change over time.

The clerk will advise the claimant of the trial date during the intake process.[117] The claimant also is entitled to certain written information explaining the process including **adjournments**, counterclaims, jury trial request, subpoena, arbitration, collection methods and fees, treble damages, and the right to notify licensors of judgments against parties who are licensed to do business.[118] Some courts hold trials at night, some during the day, and some offer both options. In New York City, trials are at night, except for persons 65 years of age and older, disabled persons, and night workers who may choose to have their trials heard during the daytime.[119] A claimant waives the right to a jury trial by commencing a small claims action.[120]

Within five days after the intake process, the clerk mails a notice of claim showing the nature of the claim, trial date, and place of trial to the defendant at the address supplied by the claimant.[121] As a practical matter, the clerk will reject any statement of claim form that does not include a local mailing address for the defendant. The notice is sent by first class mail and certified mail, return receipt requested.[122] If the notice is not returned by the Postal Service to the clerk within 21 days, it is presumed that the notice was received.[123] If, however, the clerk is not satisfied that the notice was properly delivered, the claimant is given an opportunity to complete service of the notice according to law. The law prohibits the claimant from serving the notice of claim herself. If service is not made by proper means within four months, the action is dismissed but the claimant is not prohibited from trying again.[124]

A defendant who has a claim for money against the person suing him may counterclaim in the action brought against him provided that the person suing him lives, works, or has an office in the jurisdiction.[125] The amount of the counterclaim must not exceed the amount to which the original claim is limited by law.[126] If the counterclaim exceeds that amount, the defendant may forego the excess or bring a separate action against the claimant in the appropriate court for the full amount.[127] Only the latter option is available if the counterclaim seeks any remedy other than money damages. If the defendant brings his own action in another court, the defendant may seek to join both actions through **consolidation** in that other court. Judges are particularly careful about transferring small claims to regular court because in the past some defendants abused the procedure to thwart the intent of the small claims statute and court rules. Safeguards may be imposed to protect the small claims litigant if consolidation in the higher-level court is granted.[128]

The defendant may counterclaim formally by notifying the clerk and paying a fee of $5.00 plus postage within five days of receiving notice of the claim.[129] Alternatively, the defendant may announce and file the counterclaim (with fee) on the trial date.[130] This, however, may cause the claimant to seek a postponement of the trial that he is certain to receive.[131]

The defendant is permitted to bring into the action a third party who might legally be responsible in the case.[132] The third-party action will be limited to third-party defendants who reside, work, or have an office in the court's jurisdiction.[133] The same monetary limitation applies to third-party actions as applies to ordinary claims. The claimant is permitted to sue two or more defendants in one case.[134] Any defendant may make a claim against any other defendant (**cross-claim**) who may legally be responsible to her.

Pre-trial Matters

By commencing a small claims action, a claimant is deemed to have waived a trial by jury; however, if for any reason the action is removed from the small claims part to a regular part of the court the waiver is no longer in effect.[135] A defendant, on the other hand, may demand a jury trial of a small claim by timely filing a jury demand, paying a fee (currently $70.00), making an undertaking (formal promise to pay) in the amount of $50.00 or depositing $50.00 with the court, and submitting an affidavit outlining the issues to be determined by a jury.[136] The case will then be transferred to the regular part of the court but will be tried in essentially the same manner as an ordinary small claim.[137] Jury demands are very rare.

In regular civil cases, the parties are permitted to use prescribed methods during the period leading up to the trial to acquire information about the case from each other. This is called disclosure or **discovery**.[138] Discovery is not permitted in small claims actions unless the court approves a request for it after a "showing of proper circumstances."[139] Approval rarely is given. One case where the court did approve is *Dorfman v. Bell*.[140] In the Nassau County case, an accountant was suing a doctor regarding a bill for services rendered. The doctor claimed to have tape recordings of their relevant conversations. The court ordered discovery of the tapes; the doctor had to let the claimant hear the recordings before the trial.

The making of motions (requests of the court) before trial is disapproved except in the rarest of circumstances.[141] Most litigants appear without legal representation (*pro se*) and would be confused about how to deal with motions, causing undue delay. Typically all issues can be effectively resolved at the trial without any need for pre-trial motions. Indeed, generally, even a motion made during the trial to dismiss the claim is better left undecided until after all parties are heard, or when appropriate, denied immediately.

Subpoenas are available in small claims actions.[142] A subpoena is an order to either appear and testify at a particular trial or produce physical evidence such as books and records at a trial (**subpoena *duces tecum***).[143] Parties may request subpoenas from the court clerk,[144] but they are effective only within a limited geographic area determined by law.[145] The litigant is responsible to see that the subpoena is served but may not serve the document herself.[146] Although failure to comply with a subpoena potentially subjects the subpoenaed person to contempt of court punishment,[147] adjournments permitting a second chance to comply should not be unexpected.

Trial Matters – Practice and Procedure Issues

The court is authorized by statute to establish such rules of practice and procedure for small claims as "shall constitute a simple, informal and inexpensive procedure for the prompt determination of such claims in accordance with the rules and principles of substantive law."[148] To the extent that procedural rules of the New York Supreme Court and the court to which the small claims part is attached do not conflict with the small claims rules, they too shall be applicable.[149]

A record of the proceedings is required through the taking of stenographic minutes.[150] The Uniform Rules state that the court shall "conduct the hearing in such manner as it deems best suited to discover the facts and to determine the justice of the case."[151] Some practices followed in higher-level courts typically are part of small claims procedure, viz., parties may produce witnesses and other evidence, witnesses at trial testify under oath, and direct and cross-examination of witnesses may be conducted. Most other rules of procedure and evidence applied in higher-level court need not be strictly followed. For example, **hearsay** is admissible in small claims court, although a litigant must produce some additional evidence in order to prevail.[152] Two rules of evidence do apply, however, and they render certain evidence inadmissible in court. Evidence laws "relating to privileged communications and personal transactions or communications with a decedent or a mentally ill person" apply in small claims court.[153] The former is aimed at protecting confidential relationships and the latter at excluding testimony about conversations and the like that cannot be contradicted, if untrue, because the other party to the communication is now dead or incapacitated.

A unique small claims rule describes the type of evidence admissible to prove the sum recoverable in property damage cases. The rule states: "An itemized bill or invoice, receipted or marked paid, or two itemized estimates for services or repairs, are admissible in evidence and are prima facie evidence of the reasonable value and necessity of such services and repairs."[154] This excellent rule simplifies preparation of the case by the claimant and determination of the case by the judge or arbitrator. The invoices and estimates do not have to be certified and verified as they would be if offered as evidence in higher-level proceedings.[155] The acceptance of estimates makes clear that the litigant has the option to wait until after the hearing to repair the property. Although damages may be established by other evidence, such as expert testimony, litigants who scrupulously comply with this guideline usually have success. The other party, however, may offer evidence to refute or discredit the bill or estimates proffered.

An individual litigant may represent herself or may be represented by an attorney. The judge may permit a non-attorney representative only if a party's age, mental or physical capacity, or other disability recommends it "in the interests of justice."[156] The catch is that such representative must be related to the party by "consanguinity or affinity,"[157] often interpreted to mean by blood or marriage, but open to a more liberal interpretation as to "affinity." Attorneys need not be concerned about competition for fees since "[n]o person acting as a non-attorney representative shall be permitted to charge a fee or be allowed to accept any form of remuneration for such services."[158]

Trial Matters – Substantive Issues

The legislature's prime directive to small claims courts is "to do substantial justice between the parties according to the rules of substantive law."[159] Few aspects of small claims practice have engendered as much discussion as the interplay between the terms *substantial justice* and *substantive law*. The discussion has focused on the word *substantial* and addresses the question whether its use alters what would otherwise be the court's responsibility by creating authority to bend the substantive law in the interests of a judge's vision of justice. Is a judge permitted to apply the law differently in a small claims case? Although the point is arguable,[160] the weight of authority favors a negative response; substantive law must be applied in the same way as it would in any other court. A better approach to reconciling the two terms might be to focus on the meaning of *justice* within the legal system. One of the opening quotations in this book is from the late U.S. Supreme Court Justice Potter Stewart who equated justice with fairness. The concept of justice in our courts has more to do with the fairness of the process than anything else. Perhaps the term *substantial justice* refers to procedural fairness in small claims court. It may simply be another way of saying that the litigant is not entitled to a perfect small claims trial, but only a substantially fair one, following which the substantive law will be applied. Ralph Waldo Emerson would be perplexed by the notion that substantial justice is a goal unique to small claims court. The opening quotation from Emerson reflects his belief that all good judges should do substantial justice. In any event, judicial opinions suggest that small claims litigants who are well versed in the law are likely to accurately predict the outcomes of their cases.

In the remainder of this section several laws are discussed that have been classified as substantive rather than procedural and, as such, apply in small claims court.

Statutes of limitation are laws that bar actions from court if they are not brought to court within specified time periods. The time period generally is measured from the first moment a person could have sued to the time when the person formally made the claim. They apply in all courts, including small claims courts.[161] Some of the limitation periods are: one year for most intentional torts; two years and six months for medical malpractice; three years for negligence, the tort of conversion, and legal malpractice; four years for breach of a sale of goods contract; and six years for other breaches of contract, fraud, and most other actions.[162] The many exceptions and other parts to the statute of limitations are omitted here due to space considerations and the limited scope of this book. A wise defendant will raise this issue in court if there is any chance that the limitations period expired before the claimant sued him. Winning this point means dismissal of the action.

Notice of claim laws apply in small claims court.[163] These rules typically condition the right to sue a municipality upon the giving of notice describing the claim to the municipality within ninety days after the claim arises.[164] Failure to timely deliver the notice precludes the claimant from commencing an action. A related rule that also is recognized in small claims court circumscribes the time period during which a person is permitted to sue a municipality for a tort as follows: not sooner than thirty days after proper filing of the notice of claim, but not later than one year and ninety days after the cause of action arose.[165]

The New York City pothole notification law[166] applies in small claims cases.[167] This rule bars cases against New York City that allege damage caused by potholes or certain other unsafe conditions, if the City had not been timely and properly notified of their existence before the incident.

A critically important rule called the statute of frauds applies in many contract cases in all courts, including small claims courts.[168] Refer to Chapter Three for a discussion of the rule. Defendants are advised to raise the issue of a claimant's failure to allege and produce a signed writing whenever appropriate in a contract case.

The parol evidence rule is applicable in small claims court.[169] This rule bars evidence of any alleged oral or written agreement that would contradict the express terms of a later or contemporaneously executed complete written contract between the parties involving the same transaction.[170] Parol evidence is thought to be extremely unreliable since transacting parties ordinarily include *all* agreed-upon terms in their complete, written contract.

Arbitration Option

In many small claims courts, litigants other than infants,[171] incompetent persons,[172] and conservatees[173] may choose arbitration of their claims instead of court trial. Small claim arbitrations are permitted by court rules in New York City Civil Court,[174] City Courts,[175] and District Courts,[176] but not Justice Courts. The arbitration rules are authorized by the respective Court Acts.[177] Arbitrations are conducted by volunteer attorneys appointed by the judges to assist the court. The availability of arbitration makes it much less likely that some cases scheduled for a session will be adjourned due to insufficient time to conduct all the trials. An arbitrator's services are used only if all litigants to a dispute consent with knowledge that the ruling will be final and without possibility of appeal.[178] The arbitrations are held during the same session as the trials but in different rooms. They are very similar in form to hearings before judges. They similarly end with the arbitrator making an award in each case, typically after the parties leave. Arbitrators apply the same laws as judges do in the court trials;[179] therefore, they should reach the same conclusion a judge would reach in any case, assuming they see the evidence in the same light.

Some arbitrators may seem more lenient than judges when it comes to acceptance of evidence. The Uniform Rules provide that arbitrators "shall not be bound by the rules regarding the admissibility of evidence."[180] While some judges may choose to reject evidence they deem worthless (since they are in the habit of rejecting inadmissible evidence in the regular part of the court), arbitrators may be more likely to accept the evidence "for what it's worth." This generally yields the same result, however, because even though evidence may be accepted, it always is given only such weight as the arbitrator or judge thinks it deserves.

Arbitrators do not grant adjournments; that is a judge's prerogative. Arbitrators do not conduct inquests unless they are separately appointed as **referees**.[181] No record is made of the arbitration hearing.[182] Arbitrators deliver their written decisions to the clerk who enters the judgment.[183]

Post-trial/arbitration Matters – Appeals

Generally, at the conclusion of an ordinary civil trial, any party may appeal to a higher court on the basis of not having received a fair trial. In small claims cases, however, appeals are severely restricted.

First, no appeal is permitted from a judgment based on a small claims arbitration award because parties waive all rights to appeal when they agree to arbitration[184] and the proceedings are not recorded. The courts have recognized limited grounds, however, to have the arbitration award and resulting judgment **vacated** through a motion to the trial judge. The grounds include corruption or other misconduct of the arbitrator,[185] granting of an unauthorized remedy,[186] and failure to follow important procedural rules in the arbitration.[187] Motions to vacate rarely are made or granted. Rulings on the motions may themselves be appealed to higher courts.

Second, a small claims judgment following a trial before a judge may be appealed to the same higher court that a regular claim would be, but on one ground only: "substantial justice has not been done between the parties according to the rules and principles of substantive law."[188] Appellate courts have interpreted the statutory language to mean that reversals of small claims judgments are not warranted for the type of error that suffices in other cases but require a finding that the error is shocking.[189] Appellate courts have been sufficiently shocked by small claims decisions that were clearly erroneous[190] or unsupported by competent evidence.[191] Given such a high bar for reversal, appeals are extremely difficult to win. The following cases offer two examples of rare victories.

In *DeSantis v. Sears, Roebuck and Company*,[192] a sale item was advertised by Sears department store with the inducement, "WRAP UP A BEAUTIFUL CHRISTMAS AT SEARS," but was never available during the stated time. The claimant unsuccessfully attempted to purchase the item. The claimant's case for false advertising was dismissed by small claims court. It was reinstated on appeal by an Appellate Division court that cited the *clearly erroneous* standard and found the small claims court dismissal "clearly in error given the tenor of the advertisement, which made an overture to Christmas shoppers during a limited period immediately before the holiday."[193]

In *Lockwood v. Niagara Mohawk Power Corp.*,[194] a small claims court decision against the defendant for damage caused by low-voltage power transmission was reversed by the Appellate Division because the small claims court had determined that the defendant's gross negligence caused the damage although there was no competent evidence in the record to show that. In fact, evidence in the record tended to show that the power company was not negligent at all since it reacted quickly to the storm-related problems.

A litigant pursues an appeal (and becomes the *appellant*) first by filing a notice of appeal form with the court,[195] paying a filing fee of $30.00,[196] and serving the notice on the other party within thirty days of receiving the judgment.[197] Second, the appellant must purchase, through the clerk, a typed transcript of the hearing for submission along with other required papers including written arguments supporting the appeal to the appropriate appellate court. Judgment debtors are not entitled to a **stay of execution** pending the outcome of the appeal unless they deposit into court an appropriate amount of cash or bond.[198]

Post-trial/arbitration Matters – Collection

In an effort to promote collection, the small claims court, even prior to issuing a judgment, is authorized to order examination of a defendant about her assets and restrain her from transferring them.[199] Thus, the judge may conduct a hearing about the defendant's assets immediately following the small claims trial.

The notice of judgment that is sent to the judgment creditor and judgment debtor will state when payment is due. If a judgment debtor fails to pay, the judgment creditor may use all lawful means to collect for up to twenty years.[200] If, however, the judgment debtor never possesses assets or income during that time sufficient to satisfy the judgment, there is no recourse against him. The debtor is described as *judgment proof*. The creditor may use information subpoenas to help determine whether the debtor has means to pay the judgment. These documents, which may be acquired at low cost from the court clerk,[201] may be delivered by various means including certified mail, return receipt requested, to the debtor and others who might know about his assets. They require the recipient to disclose specific information about the debtor's assets or income under threat of contempt punishment. Although such things as cars, boats, land, buildings, cash, stocks, bonds, and salary are fair game, not all of a debtor's property is available to a judgment creditor. New York State law shields certain property from collection, including part of the debtor's equity in the primary residence.[202] Collection of a judgment may lawfully be accomplished through property or income **executions of judgment**. The court clerk will advise a creditor as to the fees (currently $15.00 for a transcript of judgment) and documents needed to have an execution issued to the proper authority – a marshal or sheriff depending on which county is involved. The execution is an order to the sheriff/marshal to take property or income of the debtor to satisfy the judgment. The more information a creditor gives the sheriff/marshal about the debtor's assets and income, the more likely his efforts will be successful. The sheriff/marshal collects fees for execution. In a rather celebrated case in small claims circles, a plaintiff collected $350.00 on a default judgment from a recalcitrant debtor by execution against the debtor's $200,000.00 cooperative apartment that was sold by the sheriff for $15,000.00 to a third party.[203]

In order to encourage payment, a creditor may file a transcript of judgment with the clerk of the Supreme Court of the State of New York, increasing the likelihood that the unpaid judgment will affect the debtor's credit rating and enlarging the geographic area in which executions may be issued. The judgment also will become a lien against real property in every county in which it is appropriately filed by the creditor. The creditor may then force a sale of the real property or simply wait until the debtor decides to sell it, at which time she likely will be required to pay the judgment as a condition of closing the sale.

Two other provisions of the Court Act are designed to promote payment of small claims judgments by increasing the amount a loser is obligated to pay if he does not pay promptly in certain circumstances. First, in any case where a defendant is sued in a name other than its true name, and a judgment against it related to its business activities remains unsatisfied for thirty-five days after receipt of notice of entry, the judgment creditor is entitled to bring a second action for a revised sum equal to the amount of the original judgment, costs, reasonable attorney's fees, and an additional $100.00.[204] Even if this revised amount exceeds the small claims monetary limit, the new action may be brought in small claims court.[205] This provision discourages defendants from trying to avoid payment of judgments on the technical ground that they were not sued in their true or official name but rather in another name in which they were actually conducting business. Second, in any case where a judgment debtor has at least two previous unsatisfied small claims judgments against him arising from his business or any repeated course of conduct, and he does not pay a current judgment similarly related within thirty days of receiving a detailed warning notice, the judgment creditor may commence a new action against him for a revised sum equal to triple the amount of the unsatisfied judgment, costs, and reasonable counsel fees .[206] The new action may not be brought in small claims court, however, if the revised amount exceeds the small claims monetary limit. The debtor can defeat the new action by showing financial inability to pay the original judgment on time .[207]

Two other options are available to judgment creditors seeking collection. The first alternative is to engage the services of a private representative who will attempt to collect the judgment in exchange for a fee tied to the amount actually collected. The second alternative is to sell and assign the judgment to a private party purchaser for a negotiated price. Persons or companies engaged in such practices typically advertise their services in various media, including the Internet.

Post-trial/arbitration Matters – Miscellaneous

Small claims courts have statutory obligations to take certain actions that affect wrongdoing parties in addition to rendering judgments against them. First, whenever a claim is connected to a defendant's business, the judge or arbitrator is obligated to determine at the hearing any business or professional association to which the defendant belongs and any state or local licensing or certifying authority to which the defendant is subject.[208] If it is determined that such a defendant has committed fraudulent or illegal acts, the court must advise the licensing or certifying authority or advise the claimant to do so.[209] The small claims court clerk is required to furnish claimants with a list of prominent state and local licensing or certifying authorities and a description of the types of businesses they oversee.[210] If the fraud or illegality is demonstrated to be persistent, the court must advise the attorney general or advise the claimant to do so.[211] Second, whenever a court renders a treble damage award based on the statutory provision discussed previously, regarding a series of unpaid small claims judgments related to a defendant's business, the court must advise the attorney general, and if the defendant's business was certified or licensed, the proper authority.[212] In all licensing decisions, the authority is required to consider the licensee's deliberate or reckless failure to pay judgments.[213] Third, courts are directed to maintain under judgment debtors' names a record of unsatisfied small claims judgments against them.[214]

ANATOMY OF AN ACTION

The Claim and Related Matters

A small claim is commenced when the claimant or someone on his behalf (either one hereinafter sometimes referred to as the "filer") appears at the court for such claims, pays the clerk the required fee, and delivers the claimant's name and address, defendant's name and address, and a simple statement of the cause of action that must be reduced "to a concise written form"[215] and signed by the filer.[216] Consult the first part of this chapter for the jurisdictional and other technical details associated with commencement of the claim. The clerk must advise the filer of the hearing date.[217] The claimant will not receive a subsequent reminder of the date. The clerk is directed to schedule the hearing as soon after the claim is filed as is "practicable."[218] In New York City, the hearing will be scheduled for the evening unless the claimant requests a daytime session and is approved due to age, disability, or nighttime employment.[219] Daytime sessions are the norm or are available as of right in some locales outside New York City. The clerk is directed to provide the claimant with prescribed relevant, written information about small claims court.[220]

Within five days thereafter, the clerk will mail to the defendant, as described in the first part of this chapter, the official notice of the claim against her .[221] It will inform her of the claimant's name, nature of the claim, amount demanded, date, time, and location of the hearing, as well as certain other pertinent information regarding representation, jury trial demand, consequences of default, and the need to be prepared.[222] The defendant need not file anything with the court unless she wishes to counterclaim, **implead** an additional party or parties, desires a jury trial, or seeks an adjournment.

A defendant wishing to counterclaim should file a statement with the clerk within five days of receiving notice of the claim and pay the small fee and postage cost.[223] The clerk will then mail the notice of counterclaim to the claimant who has a right, but no obligation, to reply.[224] A defendant who fails to file the counterclaim may still present it at the hearing upon paying the fee, but will be subject to an adjournment if claimant requests one.[225] The defendant and the claimant may bring additional parties into the action as defendants by impleading them.[226] This is accomplished through the same procedures described above for the filing of the claim.[227] Limitations on counterclaims and third-party claims are discussed in the first part of this chapter.

Jury trial demands are discussed in the first part of this chapter. A defendant desiring a jury trial must file the required documents and pay all fees before the original hearing date.[228] Trials with juries are not heard in the small claims part because they would slow down the session. Instead, they are transferred to the regular part of the court, but maintain their small claims status.[229]

If after receiving notice of the claim a defendant becomes aware that he will be unavailable on the trial date, he should so notify the court and seek guidance about requesting an adjournment. Although adjournments are disfavored, usually the first one requested by a party will be granted. Should a defendant choose to ignore the notice of claim, the likely result will be a default judgment against him. Defaults are discussed later in this chapter.

Preparing for the Trial

For parties proceeding without legal representation, the next step is preparation for the trial, including organizing documentary and other evidence, securing the testimony of witnesses, and reviewing all aspects of the case to prepare an outline for the in-court presentation. Though not necessary, observing a small claims court session is another excellent way to prepare. Parties represented by counsel should prepare as directed by their counsel. Pursuant to court rules in all but the Justice Courts, when all parties have legal representation, the judge is authorized to transfer the case out of the small claims part.[230] Transfer is common since the involvement of attorneys portends a longer hearing. Sometimes, settlements are reached at this point, but since they are discussed elsewhere in this book I will not address them here. Litigants should make separate files for correspondence, other documentary evidence, and court papers. If the contents are substantial, a litigant should consider using tabs to identify the documents. A complete set of documents should be set aside for possible submission to the judge or arbitrator. Copies should be made for the opposing party. Evidence may include any relevant correspondence, contracts, leases, checks, receipts, photographs, police reports, bills, estimates, notarized statements, business records, and any physical item that is the subject of the claim, such as clothing, merchandise, and the like. For example, in a tenant's case against a landlord for return of a security deposit allegedly retained to pay for cleaning and repairs, the following evidence would be helpful to the claimant: pictures showing the condition of the premises when the tenant took possession, pictures showing the similar or better condition of the premises when the tenant vacated, the written lease, any written record of defects in the premises at the commencement or conclusion of the tenancy, receipts or similar evidence showing the purchase, by the tenant, of paint, cleaning supplies, and the like, and correspondence with the landlord about the issue.

A litigant should inform potential witnesses of the date, time, and place of the hearing to assure availability. If a crucial witness is willing to testify but is unavailable on the hearing date, the litigant should request an adjournment. Litigants are advised to discuss briefly with each witness the aspects of the case about which she will be expected to testify. Only the testimony of witnesses who have personal knowledge of relevant facts or who qualify as experts should be offered. Generally, disinterested persons make the most credible witnesses. In the hypothetical case mentioned in the preceding paragraph, the tenant should present, if possible, the testimony of one or more witnesses with first-hand knowledge of the condition of the premises. Finally, litigants should offer to drive or accompany the witnesses to the hearing to assure their presence. Witnesses other than experts may be subpoenaed. The risk associated with forcing an unwilling witness to testify must be balanced against the value of the witness to the case. Subpoenas are discussed in the first part of this chapter.

In preparing her presentation the litigant should become extremely familiar with all the facts of the case – dates, places, sequence of events. At the hearing she should be able to testify without constantly looking to documents or other aids. A litigant should be knowledgeable about the legal requirements to win the case and should structure her presentation of the facts accordingly. Drafting an outline of the points that have to be established with notations of the supporting evidence to be offered for each is helpful. For example, in a case where a building contractor was hired to install a deck, but allegedly walked off the job permanently, the claimant-homeowner's outline might look something like this:

Point One: Prove existence of contract with defendant. [Submit written contract to judge]

Point Two: Establish defendant's breach. [Testimony of contractor's disappearance halfway through job; photographs of unfinished work; contractor's phone disconnected; correspondence not answered; passage of 35 days]

Point Three: Establish amount of damages. [Submit written contract with new builder to complete the job at increased cost of $750; the increase is the amount of damages; new builder testifies as expert; photographs of finished work]

Because litigants live with their claims for months and often forget that others have not, they sometimes leave out relevant information that is familiar to them but not readily apparent. The in-court presentation must be complete or it will be incomprehensible to the judge or arbitrator who knows almost nothing about the facts associated with the claim. On the other hand, since there are many cases to be heard at the court session, concise presentations are well received.

A recurring problem for claimants is the failure to prove damages.[231] Proving that the defendant committed a wrong is not enough. Claimants must present evidence about the nature and extent of the injury or damage suffered that gives the judge or arbitrator a reasonable basis for determining the amount of money lawfully deserved. Even if the judge or arbitrator believes a claimant should win, she is not permitted to speculate as to amount of damages.[232] The topic of damages is discussed in other parts of this book.

The guiding light of case preparation as it relates to the facts is this question: What evidence would I want to see or hear that would persuade me, one way or the other, if I were an impartial judge in a case like this one involving other people? The answer should propel the litigant to prepare a winning presentation.

The Day of the Trial

All litigants should know exactly where the courthouse is and how to get there before the hearing day. Defendants, who are not likely to have visited the courthouse, are especially encouraged to heed this advice. Claimants usually know the location because most file their own claims at the courthouse.

Plan to arrive before the assigned time on the hearing day to allow for unexpected delays. Dress neatly in attire suitable for the occasion. People normally dress in their typical daily attire, which is fine unless that typical attire is dirty, torn, or otherwise inappropriate. Hats, shaded glasses, and anything else that makes the eyes and face difficult to see are discouraged. Upon arrival, check outside of the courtroom to confirm that your case is listed on the posted calendar of cases scheduled for that session. If it is not, check with the clerk immediately.

Enter the courtroom when permitted. As the time for the beginning of the session draws near a court employee will address the people about proper procedure. Listen carefully to the instructions. Each court may handle matters a little differently, so it is impossible to prepare litigants completely through this or any other book. A low divider, called the *bar*, runs across the front of the room with an opening or swinging door in it. Normally only attorneys, who are referred to as members of the *bar*, and court personnel are permitted beyond the bar. Litigants may pass across the bar when their cases are called because they have business with the court. Eventually the judge will enter and rise to the bench. One or more court officers will be present throughout the proceedings. A court reporter will take stenographic minutes unless a tape recording system is being used. The clerk will *call the calendar* of cases. When the clerk calls each case name, the claimant and defendant respond, if present, as previously instructed. Typically, litigants are told to respond either "plaintiff (or defendant) ready," if completely ready for trial or "plaintiff (or defendant) application" if not completely ready that day for any reason. Most often, applications are requests for adjournment. If there is an arbitration option available (see arbitration discussion in the first part of this chapter), but a litigant prefers a hearing in front of the judge, he should make this known at the outset when his case is called. Failure to do so may cause his case to be delivered to the arbitrator on duty.

If the defendant is not present when his case is called, the case is marked for *second call*, which refers to the time when all such cases are called again. Second call generally is made one hour after the first calendar call began. If the plaintiff does not answer the calendar call in her case, the court is authorized to dismiss the claim without prejudice to the claimant to sue again, rule in favor of the defendant in the case, or otherwise dispose of the case.[233] In between calendar calls, if there is an arbitrator on duty, all ready cases (except possibly those marked for trial in front of the judge) are sent to the arbitrator in another room. If the claimant is ready but her defendant misses first and, more than one hour later,[234] second call, the judge will hold the defendant in default and order an immediate inquest. An inquest is a hearing without the defendant present, where the claimant is expected to verify the validity of the claim and prove the amount of damages to be imposed. Either a referee (likely an arbitrator so appointed), or the judge will conduct the inquests. If the defendant shows up during the inquest it probably will be terminated in favor of a trial or arbitration. There is good news and bad news when it comes to inquests. The good news is that since an inquest is uncontested the claimant should win easily and will have up to twenty years to try to collect; the bad news is that the defendant's failure to appear probably signifies that he is not going to pay the judgment voluntarily, has left the area, has no funds, or is a defunct business entity. More bad news comes in the form of the defendant's right to request that the court vacate the default and order a trial. Although the law requires a showing of good cause for the defendant's failure to appear in order to vacate the default, many judges liberally interpret the requirement and generously grant the requests. Often the parties will be ordered to try the case on the same day that they appear to hear the judge's ruling on the motion to vacate the default.

Some cases will be settled by agreement of the parties at the courthouse prior to arbitration or trial. Any litigant whose case settles should ask for instructions from the judge, arbitrator, or clerk as to how the settlement should be formally recorded.

The conduct of the court trials and arbitrations is next addressed. Contested cases will be heard by an arbitrator if one is on duty and the parties consent. Otherwise, they will be heard by the judge. Either way, the cases are handled similarly. Depending upon the length of the calendar and where a litigant's case falls on it, the wait for a trial or arbitration may be a long one. In busier courts, judges typically postpone some trials of ready cases due to time constraints.

When called for trial, approach as directed with any witnesses. The judge or arbitrator will establish the identities of the parties and proper spellings of names. A judge may be referred to as "Your Honor;" an arbitrator as "Mr. Arbitrator," or "Ms." or "Madame Arbitrator." Nonparty witnesses other than experts may be asked to leave the room until it is time for their testimony, in order to prevent a witness who supposedly knows some facts about the case from being influenced by what he hears from other witnesses. In some courts, witnesses testify from counsel tables, in others from the witness chair or the podium. In some arbitration hearings, all involved persons sit around one big table headed by the arbitrator. In all proceedings, however, persons who testify must do so under oath or affirmation.[235] The oath is administered either individually or to all potential witnesses in a case as a group.

The hearing or arbitration generally proceeds as follows. The claimant will be asked to present her case first. This probably will include her testimony, her witnesses' testimony, and introduction of other evidence. Some judges and arbitrators, however, prefer to hear from both parties first and then any other witnesses. The defendant will be given an opportunity to cross-examine each person testifying for the claimant. Cross-examination presents a chance to ask questions that either help clarify the witness's earlier testimony or impeach the credibility of the witness by forcing him to reveal information (such as bias in favor of the other party) that reflects poorly on his credibility. Cross-examination is not an opportunity for the party to testify or argue with the witness. A litigant should decline to cross-examine if there is nothing to be gained. The judge or arbitrator may guide the person testifying or ask direct questions to keep the case on track. A LITIGANT SHOULD NOT INTERRUPT THE JUDGE OR ARBITRATOR! All questions should be answered politely. Since the judge or arbitrator has nearly unlimited power to decide the case, manners count.

Next, the defendant will be given a chance to present his case. He probably will testify in his own behalf and may offer other evidence, including the testimony of witnesses. The claimant may cross-examine.

Each party will do best if she has organized her presentation logically using the relevant law as a framework for the facts, introduced evidence at the appropriate times during her presentation, and utilized impartial witnesses to support her case whenever possible. At the conclusion of the hearing, litigants generally are told that judgment is reserved and will be mailed to them shortly. That's their cue to thank the judge or arbitrator and leave the room.

Post-trial/arbitration

If the judgment does not require any party to pay money, the matter is finally resolved unless the hearing was before a judge and an appeal is filed. Appeals are covered in the first part of this chapter. If the judgment does order the payment of money and it follows a hearing before a judge, it may be appealed. If payment is not promptly made, various lawful methods, as discussed in the first part of this chapter, are available to collect the judgment. In addition, one other method of promoting collection is available in some automobile cases. If a claim is based on the defendant's ownership or operation of a motor vehicle, the judgment is for more than $1,000.00, and it remains unpaid for 15 days, the Department of Motor Vehicles must suspend the judgment debtor's license and registration upon receipt of proper evidence of such facts.[236]

Whenever a judgment debtor pays a judgment, she should demand in exchange duplicate signed writings from the creditor acknowledging satisfaction of the judgment, one of which should be delivered to the court. Check with the court to see if there is any particular form that should be used.

Conclusion

The larger portion of this book is directed to pre-trial considerations. This suggests the truth every good trial lawyer knows about successfully litigating claims, large and small: earnest and thorough preparation is the key to success. Although victory is never a certainty, an admirable effort is ever assured by solid preparation, honesty, and respect for adversaries and the court. **Good luck!**

Endnotes

1   Time, October 20, 1958, at 24.

2   Emerson, Ralph Waldo. "The Conduct of Life (Power)" (originally published in 1860). *The Complete Works of Ralph Waldo Emerson, v. 6.* New York, NY: AMS Press, Inc., 1968. 51, 76.

3   N.Y. CITY CIV. CT. ACT (McKinney 1989 & Supp. 2011). Relevant articles are 18 and 18-A.

4   [2011] 22 N.Y.C.R.R. Part 208. Relevant sections are 208.41and 208.41-a.

5   For City Courts, see N.Y. UNIFORM CITY CT. ACT arts. 18, 18-A (McKinney 1989 & Supp. 2011); [2011] 22 N.Y.C.R.R. §§210.41, 210.41-a. For District Courts, see N.Y. UNIFORM DIST. CT. ACT arts. 18, 18-A (McKinney 1989 & Supp. 2011); [2011] N.Y.C.R.R. §§212.41, 212.41-a. For Justice Courts, see UNIFORM JUST. CT. ACT art. 18 (McKinney 1989 & Supp. 2011); [2011] 22 N.Y.C.R.R. §214.10.

6   N.Y. CITY CIV. CT. ACT §1801 (McKinney Supp. 2011). As of 2011, small claims courts may render a declaratory judgment in one type of action. *Id.* §1805(f) (McKinney Supp. 2011).

7   N.Y. CITY CIV. CT. ACT §1801 (Consol. Supp. Pam. 2011) (McKinney Supp. 2011).

8   N.Y. Uniform Just. Ct. Act §1801 (McKinney Supp. 2011).

9   Rufo v. Simpson, 86 Cal. App. 4th 573, 103 Cal. Rptr. 2d 492 (2001).

10 N.Y. GEN. OBLIG. LAW §5-703(2) (McKinney 2001).

11 N.Y. U.C.C. §2-201 (McKinney 2002).

12 N.Y. GEN. OBLIG. LAW §5-701(1) (McKinney Supp. 2011).

13 66 N.Y. Jur. 2d *Infants and Other Persons Under Legal Disability* §1 (2000).

14 *Id.* §§26, 111.

15 22 N.Y. Jur. 2d *Contracts* §§128-138, 538, 553 (2008).

16 *Id.* §§119-127.

17 N.Y. CIV. PRAC. L. & R. 3015(e) (McKinney 2010).

18 22 N.Y. Jur. 2d *Contracts* §§59-60 (2008).

19 N.Y. U.C.C. art. 2 (McKinney 2002).

[20]   *Id.* §2-205 (McKinney 2002).

[21]   *Id.* §2-201 (McKinney 2002).

[22]   *Id.* §§2-314, 2-315 (McKinney 2002).

[23]   *Id.* §2-201(1) (McKinney 2002).

[24]   *Id.* §2-201(3)(c) (McKinney 2002).

[25]   *Id.* §2-201(3)(b) (McKinney 2002).

[26]   *Id.* §2-201(2) (McKinney 2002).

[27]   *Id.* §2-201(3)(a) (McKinney 2002).

[28]   *Id.* §2-314(1) and (2) (McKinney 2002).

[29]   N.Y. GEN. BUS. LAW §218-a(3) (McKinney Supp. 2011).

[30]   Used Motor Vehicle Trade Regulation Rule, 16 C.F.R. Part 455 (2010).

[31]   Funeral Industry Practices, 16 C.F.R. Part 453 (2010).

[32]   Rule Concerning Cooling-Off Period for Sales Made at Homes or at Certain Other Locations, 16 C.F.R. Part 429 (2010).

[33]   N.Y. PERS. PROP. LAW art. 10-A (McKinney 1992 & Supp 2011).

[34]   N.Y GEN. BUS. LAW (McKinney 1996, 2004 & Supp. 2011).

[35]   *Id.* §349(a) (McKinney 2004).

[36]   *Id.* §349(h) (McKinney 2004).

[37]   *Id.*

[38]   *Id.*

[39]   *Id.*

[40]   *Id.* §389 (McKinney Supp. 2011).

[41]   *Id.* §772 (McKinney 1996).

[42]   *Id.* §350 (McKinney 2004).

[43]   *Id.* §350-a(1) (McKinney 2004).

[44]   *Id.* §350-f (McKinney 2004).

[45]   *Id.* §350-d (McKinney 2004).

[46]   *Id.* §350-e(3) (McKinney 2004).

[47]   *Id.*

[48]   *Id.*

[49]   *Id.* art. 30 (McKinney 1996 & Supp. 2011).

[50]   *Id.* §623(2) (McKinney 1996).

[51] *Id.* §624 (McKinney 1996).

[52] *Id.* §628 (McKinney 1996).

[53] *Id.* §198-a (McKinney 2004 & Supp. 2011).

[54] *Id.* §198-b (McKinney 2004).

[55] For the definition of "major household appliances," see *id.* §396-u(1)(d) (McKinney 1996).

[56] *Id.* §396-u(2) (McKinney 1996).

[57] *Id.* §396-u(7) (McKinney 1996).

[58] *Id.* art. 35-D (McKinney 1996 & Supp. 2011).

[59] *Id.* §753(1) (McKinney Supp. 2011).

[60] 36 N.Y. Jur. 2d *Damages* §33 (2005).

[61] The text alludes to the case of *Gruner & Jahr Printing and Publishing Co. v. O'Donnell*, decided on February 19, 2004 by Justice Ira Gammerman of the Supreme Court of the State of New York, County of New York. The decision is unreported but is partially quoted in the New York Times. Carr, *Judge in O'Donnell Case Rejects All Claims*, N.Y. Times, Feb. 20, 2004, at C5.

[62] 36 N.Y. Jur. 2d *Damages* §§160, 161-163 (2005).

[63] *Id.* §21.

[64] The verdict in *People v. Orenthal James Simpson* was rendered on October 3, 1995. For more information, see www.law.umkc.edu/faculty/projects/ftrials/Simpson/simpson.htm.

[65] Rufo v. Simpson, 86 Cal. App. 4th 573, 103 Cal. Rptr. 2d 492 (2001).

[66] *See generally* 60A N.Y. Jur. 2d *Fraud and Deceit* (2001).

[67] The decision is unreported, but for a discussion of the case in the local newspaper, see Salcedo, *Secret Proves Costly to Home Seller*, Newsday, September 15, 1990, at 3; *see also* Young v. Keith, 112 App. Div. 2d 625, 492 N.Y.S.2d 489 (3rd Dep't 1985). *But see* Copland v. Nathaniel, 164 Misc. 2d 507, 624 N.Y.S.2d 514 (Sup. Ct. Westchester County 1995).

[68] *See* 6A N.Y. Jur. 2d *Assault – Civil Aspects* §1 (2009).

[69] *See* 104 N.Y. Jur. 2d *Trespass* §8 (2005).

[70] N.Y. VEH. & TRAF. LAW (McKinney 1996, 2005 & Supp. 2011).

[71] 3 N.Y. Jur. 2d *Animals* §163 (2010).

[72] 9 N.Y. Jur. 2d *Bailments and Chattel Leases* §1 (2004).

[73] *Id.* §60.

[74] N.Y. GEN. OBLIG. LAW §5-325(1) (McKinney 2001).

[75] *See* 85 N.Y. Jur. 2d *Premises Liability* §1 (2001).

[76] 53 N.Y. Jur. 2d *Employment Relations* §404 (2009).

[77] N.Y. VEH. & TRAF. LAW §388 (McKinney 2005).

[78] *See* 36 N.Y. Jur. 2d *Damages* §8 (2005).

[79] *Id.* §§74-87.

[80] *Id.* §§180-182.

[81] Sharapata v. Town of Islip, 56 N.Y.2d 332, 437 N.E.2d 1104, 452 N.Y.S.2d 347 (1982).

[82] N.Y. JUD. LAW art. 21-A (McKinney 2003).

[83] N.Y. CITY CIV. CT. ACT §1802 (McKinney 1989).

[84] The Court Acts are found in volume 29-A of McKinney's Consolidated Laws of New York Annotated.

[85] N.Y. City Civ. Ct. Act §1801 (McKinney Supp. 2011).

[86] N.Y. UNIFORM JUST. CT. ACT §1801 (McKinney Supp. 2011).

[87] N.Y. City Civ. Ct. Act §1801 (McKinney Supp. 2011).

[88] 48A N.Y. Jur. 2d *Domestic Relations* §2739 (2007).

[89] N.Y. CONST. art. 6, §9.

[90] N.Y. CITY CIV. CT. ACT §1805(a) (McKinney Supp. 2011).

[91] *But see id.* §1808 (McKinney Supp. 2011).

[92] *See* Salazar v. American Export Lines, Inc., 114 N.Y.S.2d 370 (N.Y.C. Mun. Ct. N.Y. County 1952).

[93] *See* 1 N.Y. Jur. 2d *Actions* §45 (2002).

[94] N.Y. City Civ. Ct. Act §1801 (McKinney Supp. 2011).

[95] 107 Misc. 2d 938, 438 N.Y.S.2d 57 (Buffalo City Court 1981).

[96] N.Y. CITY CIV. CT. ACT §1810 (McKinney 1989).

[97] *Id.*

[98] *See id.* §1809(2) (McKinney 1989).

[99] *Id.*

[100] *Id.*

[101] *Id.* §1814 (McKinney 1989).

[102] *Id.* §1813 (McKinney 1989).

[103] *Id.* §1814(b) (McKinney 1989).

[104] *Id.* §1814(c) (McKinney 1989).

[105] *Id.* §1813(a) (McKinney 1989).

[106] *Id.* §1809(1) (McKinney 1989).

[107] Marino v. N.A.S. Plumbing & Heating Contractors, Inc., 175 Misc. 2d 519, 670 N.Y.S.2d 671 (Sup. Ct. App. T. 2d Dep't 1997)

[108] N.Y. CITY CIV. CT. ACT art. 18-A (McKinney 1989 & Supp. 2011).

[109] N.Y. UNIFORM DIST. CT. ACT art. 18-A (McKinney 1989 & Supp. 2011).

[110] N.Y. UNIFORM CITY CT. ACT art. 18-A (McKinney 1989 & Supp. 2011).

[111] N.Y. CITY CIV. CT. ACT §1801-A(b) (McKinney Supp. 2011).

[112] *Id.* §1803(a) (McKinney Supp. 2011); [2011] 22 N.Y.C.R.R. §208.41(a).

[113] N.Y. CIV. PRAC. L. & R. 1201 (McKinney 1997).

[114] N.Y. CITY CIV. CT. ACT §1803(a) (McKinney Supp. 2011).

[115] N.Y. CIV. PRAC. L. & R. 1102 (McKinney 1997).

[116] N.Y. CITY CIV. CT. ACT §1803(a) (McKinney Supp. 2011).

[117] [2011] 22 N.Y.C.R.R. §208.41(c).

[118] N.Y. CITY CIV. CT. ACT §1803(b) (McKinney Supp. 2011).

[119] *Id.* §1815 (McKinney Supp. 2011). (Two sections are designated 1815 in the statute. This is the latter one.)

[120] *Id.* §1806 (McKinney 1989).

[121] *Id.* §1803(a) (McKinney Supp. 2011); [2011] 22 N.Y.C.R.R. §208.41(d).

[122] N.Y. CITY CIV. CT. ACT §1803(a) (McKinney Supp. 2011); [2011] 22 N.Y.C.R.R. §208.41(d).

[123] N.Y. CITY CIV. CT. ACT §1803(a) (McKinney Supp. 2011).

[124] [2011] 22 N.Y.C.R.R. §208.41(g).

[125] N.Y. CITY CIV. CT. ACT §1801 (McKinney Supp. 2011).

[126] *Id.* §1805(c) (McKinney Supp. 2011).

127 *Id.*

128 *See, e.g.,* Grimm & Davis v. Goldberg, 101 Misc. 2d 829, 422 N.Y.S.2d 319 (N.Y.C. Civ. Ct. N.Y. County 1979).

129 N.Y. CITY CIV. CT. ACT §1803(c) (McKinney Supp. 2011).

130 *Id.*; [2011] 22 N.Y.C.R.R. §208.41(i).

131 N.Y. CITY CIV. CT. ACT §1803(c) (McKinney Supp. 2011); [2011] 22 N.Y.C.R.R. §208.41(i).

132 [2011] 22 N.Y.C.R.R. §208.41(k).

133 *See* Breen v. Cohen Auto Co., Inc., 75 Misc. 2d 927, 349 N.Y.S.2d 573 (Dist. Ct. Nassau County 1973).

134 [2011] 22 N.Y.C.R.R. §208.41(k).

135 N.Y. CITY CIV. CT. ACT §1806 (McKinney 1989).

136 *Id.*

137 MacCollam v. Arlington, 94 Misc. 2d 692, 405 N.Y.S.2d 204 (Albany City Ct. 1978); *see also* Javeline v. Long Island R. R., 106 Misc. 2d 814, 435 N.Y.S.2d 513 (N.Y.C. Civ. Ct. Queens County 1981).

138 *See generally* N.Y. CIV. PRAC. L. & R. art. 31 (McKinney 2005 & Supp. 2011).

139 N.Y. CITY CIV. CT. ACT §1804 (McKinney Supp. 2011).

140 86 Misc. 2d 359, 381 N.Y.S.2d 983 (Dist. Ct. Nassau County 1976).

141 *See* Cherry v. Coyne, 96 Misc. 2d 215, 408 N.Y.S.2d 937 (New Rochelle City Ct. 1978).

142 N.Y. CIV. PRAC. L. & R. 2302 (McKinney 2010).

143 *Id.* 2301 (McKinney 2010).

144 *Id.* 2302(a) (McKinney 2010).

145 *E.g.,* N.Y. CITY CIV. CT. ACT §1201 (McKinney 1989).

146 N.Y. CIV. PRAC. L. & R. 2303 (McKinney 2010).

147 *Id.* 2308 (McKinney 2010).

148 N.Y. CITY CIV. CT. ACT §1802 (McKinney 1989).

149 *Id.* §1804 (McKinney Supp. 2011).

150 *Id.* §1802 (McKinney 1989).

151 [2011] 22 N.Y.C.R.R. §208.41(j).

152 Levins v. Bucholtz, 2 App. Div. 2d 351, 155 N.Y.S.2d 770 (1ˢᵗ Dep't 1956), *aff'g* 208 Misc. 597, 145 N.Y.S.2d 79 (Sup.

Ct. App. T. 1ˢᵗ Dep't 1955).

[153] N.Y. CITY CIV. CT. ACT §1804 (McKinney Supp. 2011).

[154] *Id.*

[155] N.Y. CIV. PRAC. L. & R. 4533-a (McKinney 2007).

[156] N.Y. CITY CIV. CT. ACT §1815 (McKinney Supp. 2011). (Two sections are designated 1815 in the statute. This is the former one).

[157] *Id.*

[158] *Id.*

[159] *Id.* §1804 (McKinney Supp. 2011).

[160] *See* D. SIEGEL, NEW YORK PRACTICE §582, at 1009 (2005).

[161] *See* Cerio v. Charles Plumbing & Heating, Inc., 87 App. Div. 2d 972, 450 N.Y.S.2d 90 (4ᵗʰ Dep't 1982).

[162] N.Y. CIV. PRAC. L. & R. art. 2 (McKinney 2003).

[163] Ragosto v. Triborough Bridge & Tunnel Auth., 173 Misc. 2d 560, 663 N.Y.S.2d 462 (Sup. Ct. App. T. 1st Dep't 1997).

[164] *See, e.g.,* N.Y. GEN. MUN. LAW §50-e (McKinney Supp. 2011).

[165] N.Y. GEN. MUN. LAW §50-i (McKinney Supp. 2011).

[166] NEW YORK, N.Y., ADMIN. CODE §7-201(c)(2) (2010).

[167] Lurie v. New York City Office of Comptroller, 154 Misc. 2d 950, 587 N.Y.S.2d 831 (N.Y.C. Civ.Ct. N.Y. County 1992).

[168] Jackson v. County of Monroe Dep't of Social Services, 138 Misc. 2d 950, 525 N.Y.S.2d 986 (Monroe County Ct. 1988); *see also* Schoenfeld v. Ochsenhaut, 114 Misc.2d 585, 452 N.Y.S.2d 173 (N.Y.C. Civ. Ct. Kings County 1982) (dictum); Giummo v. Citibank, N.A., 107 Misc. 2d 895, 436 N.Y.S.2d 172 (N.Y.C. Civ. Ct. N.Y. County 1981).

[169] *See* 58 N.Y. Jur. 2d *Evidence and Witnesses* §565 (2000).

[170] *Id.* §564; N.Y. U.C.C. §2-202 (McKinney 2002).

[171] [2011] 22 N.Y.C.R.R. §208.41(n)(1).

[172] *Id.*

[173] N.Y. CIV. PRAC. L. & R. 1209 (McKinney Supp. Pam.2011).

[174] [2011] 22 N.Y.C.R.R. §208.41(n).

[175] *Id.* §210.41(m).

[176] *Id.* §212.41(m).

[177] *E.g.,* N.Y. CITY CIV. CT. ACT §1802 (McKinney 1989).

178 [2011] 22 N.Y.C.R.R. §208.41(n)(2).

179 J. GEBBIA, A GUIDE TO SMALL CLAIMS COURT 11 (2001-2002).

180 [2011] 22 N.Y.C.R.R. §208.41(n)(3).

181 For a discussion of the referee's function, see D. SIEGEL, NEW YORK PRACTICE §379 (2005).

182 [2011] 22 N.Y.C.R.R. §208.41(n)(3).

183 *Id.* §208.41(n)(5).

184 *Id.* §208.41(n)(2).

185 *See generally* D. SIEGEL, NEW YORK PRACTICE §584 (2005) (a discussion of the grounds for vacatur).

186 Scott v. Dale Carpet Cleaning, Inc., 120 Misc. 2d 118, 465 N.Y.S.2d 680 (N.Y.C. Civ. Ct. N.Y. County 1983).

187 Brown v. Burton, N.Y.L.J., Sept. 15, 1987, at 12, col. 4 (Sup. Ct. App. T. 2d Dep't).

188 N.Y. CITY CIV. CT. ACT §1807 (McKinney 1989).

189 *See* Blair v. Five Points Shopping Plaza, Inc., 51 App. Div. 2d 167, 379 N.Y.S.2d 532 (3rd Dep't 1976).

190 DeSantis v. Sears, Roebuck and Company, 148 App. Div. 2d 36, 543 N.Y.S.2d 228 (3rd Dep't 1989).

191 Rollock v. Gerald Modell Inc., 169 Misc. 2d 663, 652 N.Y.S.2d 465 (Sup. Ct. App. T. 1st Dep't 1996).

192 148 App. Div. 2d 36, 543 N.Y.S.2d 228 (3rd Dep't 1989).

193 *Id.* at 39, 543 N.Y.S.2d at 229.

194 112 App. Div. 2d 495, 491 N.Y.S.2d 211 (3rd Dep't 1985).

195 N.Y. CIV. PRAC. L. & R. 5515 (McKinney 1995).

196 N.Y. CITY CIV. CT. ACT §1911(f) (McKinney Supp. 2011).

197 N.Y. CIV. PRAC. L. & R. 5513 (McKinney Supp. 2011).

198 *Id.* 5519(2), (3) (McKinney 1995).

199 *Id.* 5229 (McKinney 1997); N.Y. CITY CIV. CT. ACT §1805(a) (McKinney Supp. 2011).

200 N.Y. CIV. PRAC. L. & R. 211(b) (McKinney 2003).

201 N.Y. CITY CIV. CT. ACT §1812(d) (McKinney Supp. 2011).

202 N.Y. CIV. PRAC. L. & R. 5206 (McKinney Supp. 2011).

203 The upholding of the sheriff's sale was affirmed without opinion on appeal. Lalor v. Taylor, 86 App. Div. 2d 782,

448 N.Y.S.2d 339 (1ˢᵗ Dep't 1982) *appeal denied*, 56 N.Y.2d 502, 450 N.Y.S.2d 1023 (1982). For a summary of events, see House v. Lalor, 119 Misc. 2d 193, 462 N.Y.S.2d 772 (Sup. Ct. N.Y. County 1983).

204 N.Y. CITY CIV. CT. ACT §1813(a) (McKinney 1989).

205 *Id.*

206 *Id.* §1812 (McKinney Supp. 2011).

207 *Id.* §1812(b) (McKinney Supp. 2011).

208 *Id.* §1804 (McKinney Supp. 2011).

209 *Id.* §1805(e) (McKinney Supp. 2011).

210 *Id.* §1803(b) (McKinney Supp. 2011).

211 *Id.* §1805(d) (McKinney Supp. 2011).

212 *Id.* §1812(c) (McKinney Supp. 2011).

213 *Id.* §1813(b) (McKinney 1989).

214 *Id.* §1811(d) (McKinney Supp. 2011).

215 *Id.* §1803(a) (McKinney Supp. 2011).

216 [2011] 22 N.Y.C.R.R. §208.41(a), (b).

217 *Id.* §208.41(c).

218 *Id.*

219 N.Y. CITY CIV. CT. ACT §1815 (McKinney Supp. 2011). (Two sections are designated 1815 in the statute. This is the latter one.)

220 *Id.* §1803(b) (McKinney Supp. 2011).

221 [2011] 22 N.Y.C.R.R. §208.41(d).

222 *Id.*

223 N.Y. CITY CIV. CT. ACT §1803(c) (McKinney Supp. 2011).

224 *Id.*

225 *Id.*; [2011] 22 N.Y.C.R.R. §208.41(i).

226 [2011] 22 N.Y.C.R.R. §208.41(k).

227 *Id.*

228 *Id.* §208.41(d).

229 MacCollam v. Arlington, 94 Misc. 2d 692, 405 N.Y.S.2d 204 (Albany City Ct. 1978); *see also* Javeline v. Long Island R. R., 106 Misc. 2d 814, 435 N.Y.S.2d 513 (N.Y.C. Civ. Ct. Queens County 1981).

[230] [2011] 22 N.Y.C.R.R. §§208.41(f), 210.41(f-1), 212.41(f-1).

[231] Webster v. Farmer, 135 Misc. 2d 12, 514 N.Y.S.2d 165 (Oswego City Ct. 1987) (dictum).

[232] *See id.*

[233] [2011] 22 N.Y.C.R.R. §208.41(j).

[234] *Id.* §208.41(h).

[235] *Id.* §§208.41(j), (n)(3); *see also* Brown v. Burton, N.Y.L.J., Sept. 15, 1987, at 12, col. 4 (Sup. Ct. App. T. 2d Dep't) (reversing lower court decision because witnesses did not give sworn testimony).

[236] N.Y. VEH. & TRAF. LAW §332 (McKinney 2005).

Appendix A

New York City Civil Court Act
Article 18 - Small Claims

Section

§ 1801. Small claims defined.

The term "small claim" or "small claims" as used in this act shall mean and include any cause of action for money only not in excess of five thousand dollars exclusive of interest and costs, or any action commenced by a party aggrieved by an arbitration award rendered pursuant to part 137 of the rules of the chief administrator of the courts (22 NYCRR Part 137) in which the amount in dispute does not exceed five thousand dollars, provided that the defendant either resides, or has an office for the transaction of business or a regular employment, within the city of New York.

§ 1802. Parts for the determination of small claims established.

The chief administrator shall assign the times and places for holding, and the judges who shall hold, one or more parts of the court in each county for the hearing of small claims as herein defined, and the rules may regulate the practice and procedure controlling the determination of such claims and prescribe and furnish the forms for instituting the same. There shall be at least one evening session of each part every month for the hearing of small claims, provided however, that the chief administrator may provide for exemption from this requirement where there exists no demonstrated need for evening sessions. Such practice, procedure and forms shall differ from the practice, procedure and forms used in the court for other than small claims, notwithstanding any provision of law to the contrary. They shall constitute a simple, informal and inexpensive procedure for the prompt determination of such claims in accordance with the rules and principles of substantive law. The procedure established pursuant to this article shall not be exclusive of but shall be alternative to the procedure now or hereafter established with respect to actions commenced in the court by the service of a summons. No rule to be enacted pursuant to this article shall dispense with or interfere with the taking of stenographic minutes of any hearing of any small claim hereunder.

§ 1803. Commencement of action upon small claim.

(a) Small claims shall be commenced upon the payment by the claimant of a filing fee of fifteen dollars for claims in the amount of one thousand dollars or less and twenty dollars for claims in the amount of more than one thousand dollars, without the service of a summons and, except by special order of the court, without the service of any pleading other than a statement of his cause of action by the claimant or someone in his behalf to the clerk, who shall reduce the same to a concise, written form and record it in a docket kept especially for such purpose. Such procedure shall provide for the sending of notice of such claim by ordinary first class mail and certified mail with return receipt requested to the party complained against at his residence, if he resides within the city of New York, and his residence is known to the claimant, or at his office or place of regular employment within the city of New York if he does not reside therein or his residence within the city of New York is not known to the claimant. If, after the expiration of twenty-one days, such ordinary first class mailing has not been returned as undeliverable, the party complained against shall be presumed to have received notice of such claim. Such notice shall include a clear description of the procedure for filing a counterclaim, pursuant to subdivision (c) of this section. Such procedure shall further provide for an early hearing upon and determination of such claim. No filing fee, however, shall be demanded or received on small claims of employees who shall comply with § 1912 (a) of this act which is hereby made applicable, except that necessary mailing costs shall be paid.

(b) The clerk shall furnish every claimant, upon commencement of the action, with information written in clear and coherent language which shall be prescribed and furnished by the office of court administration, concerning the small claims court. Such information shall include, but not be limited to, an explanation of the following terms and procedures; adjournments, counterclaims, jury trial requests, subpoenas, arbitration, collection methods and fees, the responsibility of the judgment creditor to collect data on the judgment debtor's assets, the ability of the court prior to entering judgment to order examination of or disclosure by, the defendant and restrain him, the utilization of section eighteen hundred twelve of this article concerning treble damage awards and information subpoenas including, but not limited to, specific questions to be used on information subpoenas, and the claimant's right to notify the appropriate state or local licensing or certifying authority of an unsatisfied judgment if it arises out of the carrying on, conducting or transaction of a licensed or certified business or if such business appears to be engaged in fraudulent or illegal acts or otherwise demonstrates fraud or illegality in the carrying on, conducting or transaction of its business and a list of at least the most prominent state or local licensing or certifying authorities and a description of the business categories such licensing or certifying authorities oversee. The information shall be available in English. Large signs in English shall be posted in conspicuous locations in each small claims court clerk's office, advising the public of its availability.

(c) A defendant who wishes to file a counterclaim shall do so by filing with the clerk a statement containing such counterclaim within five days of receiving the notice of claim. At the time of such filing the defendant shall pay to the clerk a filing fee of five dollars plus the cost of mailings which are required pursuant to this subdivision. The clerk shall forthwith send notice of the counterclaim by ordinary first class mail to the claimant. If the defendant fails to file the counterclaim in accordance with the provisions of this subdivision, the defendant retains the right to file the counterclaim, however the claimant may, but shall not be required to, request and obtain adjournment of the hearing to a later date. The claimant may reply to the counterclaim but shall not be required to do so.

§ 1804. Informal and simplified procedure on small claims.

The court shall conduct hearings upon small claims in such manner as to do substantial justice between the parties according to the rules of substantive law and shall not be bound by statutory provisions or rules of practice, procedure, pleading or evidence, except statutory provisions relating to privileged communications and personal transactions or communications with a decedent or mentally ill person. An itemized bill or invoice, receipted or marked paid, or two itemized estimates for services or repairs, are admissible in evidence and are prima facie evidence of the reasonable value and necessity of such services and repairs. Disclosure shall be unavailable in small claims procedure except upon order of the court on showing of proper circumstances. In every small claims action, where the claim arises out of the conduct of the defendant's business at the hearing on the matter, the judge or arbitrator shall determine the appropriate state or local licensing or certifying authority and any business or professional association of which the defendant is a member. The provisions of this act and the rules of this court, together with the statutes and rules governing supreme court practice, shall apply to claims brought under this article so far as the same can be made applicable and are not in conflict with the provisions of this article; in case of conflict, the provisions of this article shall control.

§ 1805. Remedies available; transfer of small claims.

(a) Upon determination of a small claim, the court shall direct judgment in accordance with its findings, and, when necessary to do substantial justice between the parties, may condition the entry of judgment upon such terms as the court shall deem proper. Pursuant to section fifty-two hundred twenty-nine of the civil practice law and rules, prior to entering a judgment, the court may order the examination of or disclosure by, the defendant and restrain him to the same extent as if a restraining notice had been served upon him after judgment was entered.

(b) The court shall have power to transfer any small claim or claims to any other part of the court upon such terms as the rules may provide, and proceed to hear the same according to the usual practice and procedure applicable to other parts of the court.

(c) No counterclaim shall be permitted in a small claims action, unless the court would have had monetary jurisdiction over the counterclaim if it had been filed as a small claim. Any other claim sought to be maintained against the claimant may be filed in any court of competent jurisdiction.

(d) If the defendant appears to be engaged in repeated fraudulent or illegal acts or otherwise demonstrates persistent fraud or illegality in the carrying on, conducting or transaction of business, the court shall either advise the attorney general in relation to his authority under subdivision twelve of section sixty-three of the executive law, or shall advise the claimant to do same, but shall retain jurisdiction over the small claim.

(e) If the defendant appears to be engaged in fraudulent or illegal acts or otherwise demonstrates fraud or illegality in the carrying on, conducting or transaction of a licensed or certified business, the court shall either advise the appropriate state or local licensing or certifying authority or shall advise the claimant to do same, but shall retain jurisdiction over the small claim.

(f) The court shall have the jurisdiction defined in section three thousand one of the CPLR to make a declaratory judgment with respect to actions commenced by a party aggrieved by an arbitration award rendered pursuant to part one hundred thirty-seven of the rules of the chief administrator (22 NYCRR Part 137) in which the amount in dispute does not exceed five thousand dollars.

§ 1806. Trial by jury; how obtained; discretionary costs.

A person commencing an action upon a small claim under this article shall be deemed to have waived a trial by jury, but if said action shall be removed to a regular part of the court, the plaintiff shall have the same right to demand a trial by jury as if such action had originally been begun in such part. Any party to such action, other than the plaintiff, prior to the day upon which he is notified to appear or answer, may file with the court a demand for a trial by jury and his affidavit that there are issues of fact in the action requiring such a trial, specifying the same and stating that such trial is desired and intended in good faith. Such demand and affidavit shall be accompanied with the jury fee required by law and an undertaking in the sum of fifty dollars in such form as may be approved by the rules, payable to the other party or parties, conditioned upon the payment of any costs which may be entered against him in the said action or any appeal within thirty days after the entry thereof; or, in lieu of said undertaking, the sum of fifty dollars may be deposited with the clerk of the court and thereupon the clerk shall forthwith transmit such original papers or duly attested copies thereof as may be provided by the rules to the part of the court to which the action shall have been transferred and assigned and such part may require pleadings in such action as though it had been begun by the service of a summons. Such action may be considered a preferred cause of action. In any small claim which may have been transferred to another part of the court, the court may award costs up to twenty-five dollars to the plaintiff if he prevails.

§ 1807. Review.

A person commencing an action upon a small claim under this article shall be deemed to have waived all right to appeal, except that either party may appeal on the sole grounds that substantial justice has not been done between the parties according to the rules and principles of substantive law.

§ 1808. Judgment obtained to be res judicata in certain cases.

A judgment obtained under this article shall not otherwise be deemed an adjudication of any fact at issue or found therein in any other action or court; except that a subsequent judgment obtained in another action or court involving the same facts, issues and parties shall be reduced by the amount of a judgment awarded under this article.

§ 1809. Procedures relating to corporations, associations, insurers and assignees.

1. No corporation, except a municipal corporation, public benefit corporation, school district or school district public library wholly or partially within the municipal corporate limit, no partnership, or association and no assignee of any small claim shall institute an action or proceeding under this article, nor shall this article apply to any claim or cause of action brought by an insurer in its own name or in the name of its insured whether before or after payment to the insured on the policy.

2. A corporation may appear in the defense of any small claim action brought pursuant to this article by an attorney as well as by any authorized officer, director or employee of the corporation provided that the appearance by a non-lawyer on behalf of a corporation shall be deemed to constitute the requisite authority to bind the corporation in a settlement or trial. The court or arbitrator may make reasonable inquiry to determine the authority of any person who appears for the corporation in defense of a small claims court case.

§ 1810. Limitation on right to resort to small claims procedures.

If the clerk shall find that the procedures of the small claims part are sought to be utilized by a claimant for purposes of oppression or harassment, as where a claimant has previously resorted to such procedures on the same claim and has been unsuccessful after the hearing thereon, the clerk may in his discretion compel the claimant to make application to the court for leave to prosecute the claim in the small claims part. The court upon such application may inquire into the circumstances and, if it shall find that the claim has already been adjudicated, or that the claim is sought to be brought on solely for purposes of oppression or harassment and not under color of right, it may make an order denying the claimant the use of the small claims part to prosecute the claim.

§ 1811. Notice of small claims judgments and indexing of unpaid claims.

(a) Notice of judgment sent to judgment debtor shall specify that a failure to satisfy a judgment may subject the debtor to any one or combination of the following actions:

1. garnishment of wage;
2. garnishment of bank account;
3. a lien on personal property;
4. seizure and sale of real property;
5. seizure and sale of personal property, including automobiles;

6. suspension of motor vehicle license and registration, if claim is based on defendant's ownership or operation of a motor vehicle;

7. revocation, suspension, or denial of renewal of any applicable business license or permit;

8. investigation and prosecution by the attorney general for fraudulent or illegal business practices; and

9. a penalty equal to three times the amount of the unsatisfied judgment plus attorney's fees, if there are other unpaid claims.

(b) Notice of judgment sent to judgment creditor shall contain but not be limited to the following information:

1. the claimant's right to payment within thirty days following the debtor's receipt of the judgment notice;

2. the procedures for use of section eighteen hundred twelve of this article concerning the identification of assets of the judgment debtor, including the use of information subpoenas, access to consumer credit reports and the role of sheriffs and marshals, and actions to collect three times the judgment award and attorney's fees if there are two other unsatisfied claims against the debtor;

3. the claimant's right to initiate actions to recover the unpaid judgment through the sale of the debtor's real property, or personal property;

4. the claimant's right to initiate actions to recover the unpaid judgment through suspension of debtor's motor vehicle license and registration, if claim is based on defendant's ownership or operation of a motor vehicle;

5. the claimant's right to notify the appropriate state or local licensing or certifying authority of an unsatisfied judgment as a basis for possible revocation, suspension, or denial of renewal of business license; and

6. a statement that upon satisfying the judgment, the judgment debtor shall present appropriate proof thereof to the court; and

7. the claimant's right to notify the attorney general if the debtor is a business and appears to be engaged in fraudulent or illegal business practices.

(c) Notice of judgment sent to each party shall include the following statement: "An appeal from this judgment must be taken no later than the earliest of the following dates: (i) thirty days after receipt in court of a copy of the judgment by the appealing party, (ii) thirty days after personal delivery of a copy of the judgment by another party to the action to the appealing party (or by the appealing party to another party), or (iii) thirty-five days after the mailing of a copy of the judgment to the appealing party by the clerk of the court or by another party to the action."

(d) All wholly or partially unsatisfied small claims court judgments shall be indexed alphabetically and chronologically under the name of the judgment debtor. Upon satisfying the judgment, the judgment debtor shall present appropriate proof to the court and the court shall indicate such in the records.

§ 1812. Enforcement of small claims judgments.

(a) The special procedures set forth in subdivision (b) hereof shall be available only where: 1. there is a recorded judgment of a small claims court; and 2. (i) the aforesaid judgment resulted from a transaction in the course of the trade or business of the judgment debtor, or arose out of a repeated course of dealing or conduct of the judgment debtor, and (ii) there are at least two other unsatisfied recorded judgments of a small claims court arising out of such trade or business or repeated course of dealing or conduct, against that judgment debtor; and 3. the judgment debtor failed to satisfy such judgment within a period of thirty days after receipt of notice of such judgment. Such notice shall be given in the same manner as provided for the service of a summons or by certified mail, return receipt requested, and shall contain a statement that such judgment exists, that at least two other unsatisfied recorded judgments exist, and that failure to pay such judgment may be the basis for an action, for treble the amount of such unsatisfied judgment, pursuant to this section.

(b) Where each of the elements of subdivision (a) of this section are present the judgment creditor shall be entitled to commence an action against said judgment debtor for treble the amount of such unsatisfied judgment, together with reasonable counsel fees, and the costs and disbursements of such action, provided, however, that in any such action it shall be a defense that the judgment debtor did not have resources to satisfy such judgment within a period of thirty days after receipt of notice of such judgment. The failure to pay a judgment obtained in an action pursuant to this section shall not be the basis for another such action pursuant to this section.

(c) Where the judgment is obtained in an action pursuant to subdivision (b), and arises from a business of the defendant, the court shall, in addition to its responsibilities under this article, advise the attorney general in relation to his authority under subdivision twelve of section sixty-three of the executive law, and if such judgment arises from a certified or licensed business of the defendant, advise the state or local licensing or certifying authority.

(d) Where a judgment has been entered in a small claims court and remains unsatisfied, the small claims clerk shall, upon request, issue information subpoenas, at nominal cost, for the judgment creditor and provide the creditor with assistance on their preparation and use. The court shall have the same power as the supreme court to punish a contempt of court committed with respect to an information subpoena.

§ 1813. Duty to pay judgments.

(a) Any person, partnership, firm or corporation which is sued in a small claims court for any cause of action arising out of its business activities, shall pay any judgment rendered against it in its true name or in any name in which it conducts business. "True name" includes the legal name of a natural person and the name under which a partnership, firm or corporation is licensed, registered, incorporated or otherwise authorized to do business. "Conducting business" as used in this section shall include, but not be limited to, maintaining signs at business premises or on business vehicles; advertising; entering into contracts; and printing or using sales slips, checks, invoices or receipts. Whenever a judgment has been rendered against a person, partnership, firm or corporation in other than its true name and the judgment has remained unpaid for thirty-five days after receipt by the judgment debtor of notice of its entry, the aggrieved judgment creditor shall be entitled to commence an action in small claims court or in any other court of otherwise competent jurisdiction against such judgment debtor, notwithstanding the jurisdictional limit of the court, for the sum of the original judgment, costs, reasonable attorney's fees, and one hundred dollars.

(b) Whenever a judgment which relates to activities for which a license is required has been rendered against a business which is licensed by a state or local licensing authority and which remains unpaid for thirty-five days after receipt by the judgment debtor of notice of its entry and the judgment has not been stayed or appealed, the state or local licensing authority shall consider such failure to pay if deliberate or part of a pattern of similar conduct indicating recklessness, as a basis for the revocation, suspension, conditioning or refusal to grant or renew such license. Nothing herein shall be construed to preempt an authority's existing policy if it is more restrictive.

(c) The clerk shall attach to the notice of suit required under this article a notice of the duty imposed by this section.

§ 1814. Designation of defendant; amendment procedure.

(a) A party who is ignorant, in whole or in part, of the true name of a person, partnership, firm or corporation which may properly be made a party defendant, may proceed against such defendant in any name used by the person, partnership, firm or corporation in conducting business, as defined in subdivision (a) of section eighteen hundred thirteen of this article.

(b) If the true name of the defendant becomes known at any time prior to the hearing on the merits, such information shall be brought to the attention of the clerk, who shall immediately amend all prior proceedings and papers. The clerk shall send an amended notice to the defendant, without payment of additional fees by the plaintiff, and all subsequent proceedings and papers shall be amended accordingly.

(c) In every action in the small claims part, at the hearing on the merits, the judge or arbitrator shall determine the defendant's true name. The clerk shall amend all prior proceedings and papers to conform to such determination, and all subsequent proceedings and papers shall be amended accordingly.

(d) A party against whom a judgment has been entered pursuant to this article, in any proceeding under section five thousand fifteen of the civil practice law and rules for relief from such judgment, shall, disclose its true name; any and all names in which it is conducting business; and any and all names in which it was conducting business at the time of the transaction or occurrence on which such judgment is based. All subsequent proceedings and papers shall be amended to conform to such disclosure.

*§ 1815.   Appearance by non-attorney representatives.

The court may permit, upon the request of a party, that a non-attorney representative, who is related by consanguinity or affinity to such party, be allowed to appear on behalf of such party when the court finds that due to the age, mental or physical capacity or other disability of such party that it is in the interests of justice to permit such representation. No person acting as a non-attorney representative shall be permitted to charge a fee or be allowed to accept any form of remuneration for such services.

---

*There are 2 sections numbered "1815."

**§ 1815.   Access to daytime pro se part.

1. Senior citizens, disabled persons and members of the work force whose normal work schedule requires them to work during evening hours may institute a small claims action or proceeding returnable to the daytime pro se part of the court.

2. The clerk of the court shall verbally inform all claimants who appear to qualify or who submit adequate documentation, upon commencement of the small claims action, of the right to have any small claims heard in the daytime pro se part upon such terms as provided herein. Notwithstanding any inconsistent provision of law, a claimant shall have the right upon presenting proof to the clerk that he is sixty-five years of age or older, that he is disabled as defined in subdivision twenty-one of section two hundred ninety-two of the executive law or that he is employed in a capacity which requires him to work during evening hours and the court shall proceed to hear the case according to the practice and procedure applicable to the small claims part.

3. The clerk of the court shall publicize the availability of such forum. Such publicity shall include but not be limited to prerecorded taped messages and large signs in English and Spanish to be posted in conspicuous locations in each small claims court clerk's office, advising the public of the availability.

**There are 2 sections numbered "1815."

Appendix B

New York City Civil Court Act
Article 18-A - Commercial Claims

§ 1801-A. Commercial claims defined.

(a) The term "commercial claim" or "commercial claims" as used in this article shall mean and include any cause of action for money only not in excess of the maximum amount permitted for a small claim in the small claims part of the court, exclusive of interest and costs, provided that subject to the limitations contained in section eighteen hundred nine-A of this article, the claimant is a corporation, partnership or association, which has its principal office in the state of New York and provided that the defendant either resides, or has an office for the transaction of business or a regular employment, within the city of New York.

(b) Consumer transaction defined. The term "consumer transaction" means a transaction between a claimant and a natural person, wherein the money, property or service which is the subject of the transaction is primarily for personal, family or household purposes.

§ 1802-A. Parts for the determination of commercial claims established.

The chief administrator shall assign the times and places for holding, and the judges who shall hold, one or more parts of the court in each county for the hearing of commercial claims as herein defined, and the rules may regulate the practice and procedure controlling the determination of such claims and prescribe and furnish the forms for instituting the same. There shall be at least one evening session of each part every month for the hearing of commercial claims, provided however, that the chief administrator may provide for exemption from this requirement where there exists no demonstrated need for evening sessions. The chief administrator shall not combine commercial claims part actions with small claims part actions for purposes of convenience unless a preference is given to small claims and to commercial claims arising out of consumer transactions. Such practice, procedure and forms shall differ from the practice, procedure and forms used in the court for other than small claims and commercial claims, notwithstanding any provision of law to the contrary. They shall constitute a simple, informal and inexpensive procedure for the prompt determination of commercial claims in accordance with the rules and principles of substantive law. The procedure established pursuant to this article shall not be exclusive of but shall be alternative to the procedure now or hereafter established with respect to actions commenced in the court by the service of a summons. No rule to be enacted pursuant to this article shall dispense with or interfere with the taking of stenographic minutes of any hearing of any commercial claim hereunder.

§ 1803-A. Commencement of action upon commercial claim.

(a) Commercial claims other than claims arising out of consumer transactions shall be commenced upon the payment by the claimant of a filing fee of twenty-five dollars and the cost of mailings as herein provided, without the service of a summons and, except by special order of the court, without the service of any pleading other than a required certification verified as to its truthfulness by the claimant on a form prescribed by the state office of court administration and filed with the clerk, that no more than five such actions or proceedings (including the instant action or proceeding) have been instituted during that calendar month, and a required statement of its cause of action by the claimant or someone in its behalf to the clerk, who shall reduce the same to a concise, written form and record it in a docket kept especially for such purpose. Such procedure shall provide that the commercial claims part of the court shall have no jurisdiction over, and shall dismiss, any case with respect to which the required certification is not made upon the attempted institution of the action or proceeding. Such procedure shall provide for the sending of notice of such claim by ordinary first class mail and certified mail with return receipt requested to the party complained against at his residence, if he resides within the city of New York, and his residence is known to the claimant, or at his office or place of regular employment within the city of New York if he does not reside therein or his residence within the city of New York is not known to the claimant. If, after the expiration of twenty-one days, such ordinary first class mailing has not been returned as undeliverable, the party complained against shall be presumed to have received notice of such claim. Such notice shall include a clear description of the procedure for filing a counterclaim, pursuant to subdivision (d) of this section. Such procedure shall further provide for an early hearing upon and determination of such claim. The hearing shall be scheduled in a manner which, to the extent possible, minimizes the time the party complained against must be absent from employment. Either party may request that the hearing be scheduled during evening hours, provided that the hearing shall not be scheduled during evening hours if it would cause unreasonable hardship to either party. The court shall not unreasonably deny requests for evening hearings if such requests are made by the claimant upon commencement of the action or by the party complained against within fourteen days of receipt of the notice of claim.

(b) Commercial claims in actions arising out of consumer transactions shall be commenced upon the payment by the claimant of a filing fee of twenty-five dollars and the cost of mailings as herein provided, without the service of a summons and, except by special order of the court, without the service of any pleading other than a required statement of the cause of action by the claimant or someone on its behalf of the clerk, who shall reduce the same to a concise written form including the information required by subdivision (c) of this section, denominate it conspicuously as a consumer transaction, and record it in the docket marked as a consumer transaction, and by filing with the clerk a required certificate verified as to its truthfulness by the claimant on forms prescribed by the state office of court administration. Such verified certificate shall certify (i) that the claimant has mailed by ordinary first class mail to the party complained against a demand letter, no less than ten days and no more than one hundred eighty days prior to the commencement of the claim, and (ii) that, based upon information and belief, the claimant has not instituted more than five actions or proceedings (including the instant action or proceeding) during the calendar month. A form for the demand letter shall be prescribed and furnished by the state office of court administration and shall require the following information: the date of the consumer transaction; the amount that remains unpaid; a copy of the original debt instrument or other document underlying the debt and an accounting of all payments, and, if the claimant was not a party to the original transaction, the names and addresses of the parties to the original transaction; and a statement that the claimant intends to use this part of the court to obtain a judgment, that further notice of a hearing date will be sent, unless payment is received by a specified date, and that the party complained against will be entitled to appear at said hearing and present any defenses to the claim. In the event that the verified certificate is not properly completed by the claimant, the court shall not allow the action to proceed until the verified certificate is corrected. Notice of such claim shall be sent by the clerk by both ordinary first class mail and certified mail with return receipt requested to the party complained against at his residence, if he resides within the city of New York, and his residence is known to the claimant, or at his office or place of regular employment within the city of New York if he does not reside therein or his residence within the city of New York is not known to the claimant. If, after the expiration of thirty days, such ordinary first class mailing has not been returned as undeliverable, the party complained against shall be presumed to have received notice of such claim. Such procedure shall further provide for an early hearing upon and determination of such claim. The hearing shall be scheduled in a manner which, to the extent possible, minimizes the time the party complained against must be absent from employment. Either party may request that the hearing be scheduled during evening hours, provided that the hearing shall not be scheduled during evening hours if it would cause unreasonable hardship to either party. The court shall not unreasonably deny requests for evening hearings if such requests are made by the claimant upon commencement of the action or by the party complained against within fourteen days of receipt of the notice of claim.

(c) The clerk shall furnish every claimant, upon commencement of the action, and every party complained against, with the notice of claim, and with information written in clear and coherent language which shall be prescribed and furnished by the state office of court administration, concerning the commercial claims part. Such information shall include, but not be limited to, the form for certification and filing by the claimant that no more than five such actions or proceedings have been instituted during that calendar month, and an explanation of the following terms and procedures: adjournments, counterclaims, jury trial requests, evening hour requests, demand letters in cases concerning consumer transactions, default judgments, subpoenas, arbitration and collection methods, the responsibility of the judgment creditor to collect data on the judgment debtor's assets, the ability of the court prior to entering judgment to order examination of or disclosure by, the defendant and restrain him, and a statement in Spanish that such information is available in Spanish upon request. The information shall be available in English and Spanish. Large signs in English and Spanish shall be posted in conspicuous locations in each commercial claims part clerk's office, advising the public of its availability.

(d) A defendant who wishes to file a counterclaim shall do so by filing with the clerk a statement containing such counterclaim within five days of receiving the notice of claim. At the time of such filing the defendant shall pay to the clerk a filing fee of five dollars plus the cost of mailings which are required pursuant to this subdivision. The clerk shall forthwith send notice of the counterclaim by ordinary first class mail to the claimant. If the defendant fails to file the counterclaim in accordance with the provisions of this subdivision, the defendant retains the right to file the counterclaim, however the claimant may, but shall not be required to, request and obtain adjournment of the hearing to a later date. The claimant may reply to the counterclaim but shall not be required to do so.

§ 1804-A. Informal and simplified procedure on commercial claims.

The court shall conduct hearings upon commercial claims in such manner as to do substantial justice between the parties according to the rules of substantive law and shall not be bound by statutory provisions or rules of practice, procedure, pleading or evidence, except statutory provisions relating to privileged communications and personal transactions or communications with a decedent or mentally ill person. An itemized bill or invoice, receipted or marked paid, or two itemized estimates for services or repairs, are admissible in evidence and are prima facie evidence of the reasonable value and necessity of such services and repairs. Disclosure shall be unavailable in commercial claims procedure except upon order of the court on showing of proper circumstances. The provisions of this act and the rules of this court, together with the statutes and rules governing supreme court practice, shall apply to claims brought under this article so far as the same can be made applicable and are not in conflict with the provisions of this article; in case of conflict, the provisions of this article shall control.

§ 1805-A. Remedies available; transfer of commercial claims.

(a) Upon determination of a commercial claim, the court shall direct judgment in accordance with its findings, and, when necessary to do substantial justice between the parties, may condition the entry of judgment upon such terms as the court shall deem proper. Pursuant to section fifty-two hundred twenty-nine of the civil practice law and rules, prior to entering a judgment, the court may order the examination of or disclosure by, the defendant and restrain him to the same extent as if a restraining notice had been served upon him after judgment was entered.

(b) The court shall have power to transfer any commercial claim or claims to any other part of the court upon such terms as the rules may provide, and proceed to hear the same according to the usual practice and procedure applicable to other parts of the court.

(c) No counterclaim shall be permitted in a commercial claims action, unless the court would have had monetary jurisdiction over the counterclaim if it had been filed as a commercial claim. Any other claim sought to be maintained against the claimant may be filed in any court of competent jurisdiction.

§ 1806-A. Trial by jury; how obtained; discretionary costs.

A claimant commencing an action upon a commercial claim under this article shall be deemed to have waived a trial by jury, but if said action shall be removed to a regular part of the court, the claimant shall have the same right to demand a trial by jury as if such action had originally been begun in such part. Any party to such action, other than the claimant, prior to the day upon which he is notified to appear or answer, may file with the court a demand for a trial by jury and his affidavit that there are issues of fact in the action requiring such a trial, specifying the same and stating that such trial is desired and intended in good faith. Such demand and affidavit shall be accompanied with the jury fee required by law and an undertaking in the sum of fifty dollars in such form as may be approved by the rules, payable to the other party or parties, conditioned upon the payment of any costs which may be entered against him in the said action or any appeal within thirty days after the entry thereof; or, in lieu of said undertaking, the sum of fifty dollars may be deposited with the clerk of the court and thereupon the clerk shall forthwith transmit such original papers or duly attested copies thereof as may be provided by the rules to the part of the court to which the action shall have been transferred and assigned and such part may require pleadings in such action as though it had been begun by the service of a summons. Such action may be considered a preferred cause of action. In any commercial claim which may have been transferred to another part of the court, the court may award costs up to twenty-five dollars to the claimant if the claimant prevails.

§ 1807-A. Proceedings on default and review of judgments.

(a) A claimant commencing an action upon a commercial claim under this article shall be deemed to have waived all right to appeal, except that either party may appeal on the sole grounds that substantial justice has not been done between the parties according to the rules and principles of substantive law.

(b) The clerk shall mail notice of the default judgment by first class mail, both to the claimant and to the party complained against. Such notice shall inform the defaulting party, in language promulgated by the state office of court administration, of such party's legal obligation to pay; that failure to pay may result in garnishments, repossessions, seizures and similar actions; and that if there was a reasonable excuse for the default, the defaulting party may apply to have the default vacated by submitting a written request to the court.

(c) Proceedings on default under this article are to be governed by, but are not limited to, section five thousand fifteen of the civil practice law and rules.

§ 1808-A. Judgment obtained to be res judicata in certain cases.

A judgment obtained under this article shall not otherwise be deemed an adjudication of any fact at issue or found therein in any other action or court; except that a subsequent judgment obtained in another action or court involving the same facts, issues and parties shall be reduced by the amount of a judgment awarded under this article.

§ 1809-A. Procedures relating to corporations, associations, insurers and assignees.

(a) Any corporation, including a municipal corporation or public benefit corporation, partnership, or association, which has its principal office in the city of New York and an assignee of any commercial claim may institute an action or proceeding under this article.

(b) No person or co-partnership, engaged directly or indirectly in the business of collection and adjustment of claims, and no corporation or association, directly or indirectly, itself or by or through its officers, agents or employees, shall solicit, buy or take an assignment of, or be in any manner interested in buying or taking an assignment of a bond, promissory note, bill of exchange, book debt, or other thing in action, or any claim or demand, with the intent and for the purpose of bringing an action or proceeding thereon under this article.

(c) A corporation, partnership or association, which institutes an action or proceeding under this article shall be limited to five such actions or proceedings per calendar month. Such corporation, partnership or association shall complete and file with the clerk the required certification, provided it is true and verified as to its truthfulness, as a prerequisite to the institution of an action or proceeding in this part of the court.

(d) A corporation may appear as a party in any action brought pursuant to this article by an attorney as well as by any authorized officer, director or employee of the corporation provided that the appearance by a non-lawyer on behalf of a corporation shall be deemed to constitute the requisite authority to bind the corporation in a settlement or trial. The court or arbitrator may make reasonable inquiry to determine the authority of any person who appears for the corporation in a commercial claims part case.

§ 1810-A. Limitation on right to resort to commercial claims procedures.

If the clerk shall find that the procedures of the commercial claims part are sought to be utilized by a claimant for purposes of oppression or harassment, as where a claimant has previously resorted to such procedures on the same claim and has been unsuccessful after the hearing thereon, the clerk may in his discretion compel the claimant to make application to the court for leave to prosecute the claim in the commercial claims part. The court upon such application may inquire into the circumstances and, if it shall find that the claim has already been adjudicated, or that the claim is sought to be brought on solely for purposes of oppression or harassment and not under color of right, it may make an order denying the claimant the use of the commercial claims part to prosecute the claim.

§ 1811-A. Indexing commercial claims part judgments.

All wholly or partially unsatisfied commercial claims part judgments shall be indexed alphabetically and chronologically under the name of the judgment debtor. Upon satisfying the judgment, the judgment debtor shall present appropriate proof to the court and the court shall indicate such in the records.

§ 1812-A. Enforcement of commercial claims judgments.

Where a judgment has been entered in a commercial claims part and remains unsatisfied, the commercial claims clerk shall, upon request, issue information subpoenas, at nominal cost, for the judgment creditor and provide the creditor with assistance on their preparation and use.

§ 1813-A. Duty to pay judgments.

(a) Any person, partnership, firm or corporation which is sued in a commercial claims part for any cause of action arising out of its business activities, shall pay any judgment rendered against it in its true name or in any name in which it conducts business. "True name" includes the legal name of a natural person and the name under which a partnership, firm or corporation is licensed, registered, incorporated or otherwise authorized to do business. "Conducting business" as used in this section shall include, but not be limited to, maintaining signs at business premises or on business vehicles; advertising; entering into contracts; and printing or using sales slips, checks, invoices or receipts. Whenever a judgment has been rendered against a person, partnership, firm or corporation in other than its true name and the judgment has remained unpaid for thirty-five days after receipt by the judgment debtor of notice of its entry, the aggrieved judgment creditor shall be entitled to commence an action in commercial claims part or in any other court of otherwise competent jurisdiction against such judgment debtor, notwithstanding the jurisdictional limit of the court, for the sum of the original judgment, costs, reasonable attorney's fees, and one hundred dollars.

(b) Whenever a judgment which relates to activities for which a license is required has been rendered against a business which is licensed by a state or local licensing authority and which remains unpaid for thirty-five days after receipt by the judgment debtor of notice of its entry and the judgment has not been stayed or appealed, the state or local licensing authority shall consider such failure to pay if deliberate or part of a pattern of similar conduct indicating recklessness, as a basis for the revocation, suspension, conditioning or refusal to grant or renew such license. Nothing herein shall be construed to preempt an authority's existing policy if it is more restrictive.

(c) The clerk shall attach to the notice of suit required under this article a notice of the duty imposed by this section.

§ 1814-A. Designation of defendant; amendment procedure.

(a) A party who is ignorant, in whole or in part, of the true name of a person, partnership, firm or corporation which may properly be made a party defendant, may proceed against such defendant in any name used by the person, partnership, firm or corporation in conducting business, as defined in subdivision (a) of section eighteen hundred thirteen-A of this article.

(b) If the true name of the defendant becomes known at any time prior to the hearing on the merits, such information shall be brought to the attention of the clerk, who shall immediately amend all prior proceedings and papers. The clerk shall send an amended notice to the defendant, without payment of additional fees by the plaintiff, and all subsequent proceedings and papers shall be amended accordingly.

(c) In every action in the commercial claims part, at the hearing on the merits, the judge or arbitrator shall determine the defendant's true name. The clerk shall amend all prior proceedings and papers to conform to such determination, and all subsequent proceedings and papers shall be amended accordingly.

(d) A party against whom a judgment has been entered pursuant to this article, in any proceeding under section five thousand fifteen of the civil practice law and rules for relief from such judgment, shall disclose its true name; any and all names in which it is conducting business; and any and all names in which it was conducting business at the time of the transaction or occurrence on which such judgment is based. All subsequent proceedings and papers shall be amended to conform to such disclosure.

Appendix C

Uniform District Court Act
Article 18 - Small Claims

§ 1801. Small claims defined.

The term "small claim" or "small claims" as used in this act shall mean and include any cause of action for money only not in excess of five thousand dollars exclusive of interest and costs, or any action commenced by a party aggrieved by an arbitration award rendered pursuant to part one hundred thirty-seven of the rules of the chief administrator of the courts (22 NYCRR Part 137) in which the amount in dispute does not exceed five thousand dollars, provided that the defendant either resides, or has an office for the transaction of business or a regular employment, within a district of the court in the county.

§ 1802. Parts for the determination of small claims established.

The chief administrator shall assign the times and places for holding, and the judges who shall hold, one or more parts of the court for the hearing of small claims as herein defined, and the rules may regulate the practice and procedure controlling the determination of such claims and prescribe and furnish the forms for instituting the same. There shall be at least one evening session of each part every month for the hearing of small claims, provided however, that the chief administrator may provide for exemption from this requirement where there exists no demonstrated need for evening sessions. Such practice, procedure and forms shall differ from the practice, procedure and forms used in the court for other than small claims, notwithstanding any provision of law to the contrary. They shall constitute a simple, informal and inexpensive procedure for the prompt determination of such claims in accordance with the rules and principles of substantive law. The procedure established pursuant to this article shall not be exclusive of but shall be alternative to the procedure now or hereafter established with respect to actions commenced in the court by the service of a summons. No rule to be enacted pursuant to this article shall dispense with or interfere with the taking of stenographic minutes of any hearing of any small claim hereunder.

§ 1803. Commencement of action upon small claim.

(a) Small claims shall be commenced upon the payment by the claimant of a filing fee of fifteen dollars for claims in the amount of one thousand dollars or less and twenty dollars for claims in the amount of more than one thousand dollars, without the service of a summons and, except by special order of the court, without the service of any pleading other than a statement of his cause of action by the claimant or someone in his behalf to the clerk, who shall reduce the same to a concise, written form and record it in a docket kept especially for such purpose. Such procedure shall provide for the sending of notice of such claim by ordinary first class mail and certified mail with return receipt requested to the party complained against at his residence, if he resides within a district of the court in the county, and his residence is known to the claimant, or at his office or place of regular employment within such a district if he does not reside therein or his residence within such a district is not known to the claimant. If, after the expiration of twenty-one days, such ordinary first class mailing has not been returned as undeliverable, the party complained against shall be presumed to have received notice of such claim. Such notice shall include a clear description of the procedure for filing a counterclaim, pursuant to subdivision (c) of this section. Such procedure shall further provide for an early hearing upon and determination of such claim. No filing fee, however, shall be demanded or received on small claims of employees who shall comply with § 1912 (a) of this act which is hereby made applicable, except that necessary mailing costs shall be paid.

(b) The clerk shall furnish every claimant, upon commencement of the action, with information written in clear and coherent language which shall be prescribed and furnished by the office of court administration, concerning the small claims court. Such information shall include, but not be limited to, an explanation of the following terms and procedures; adjournments, counterclaims, jury trial requests, subpoenas, arbitration, collection methods and fees, the responsibility of the judgment creditor to collect data on the judgment debtor's assets, the ability of the court prior to entering judgment to order examination of or disclosure by, the defendant and restrain him, the utilization of section eighteen hundred twelve of this article concerning treble damage awards and information subpoenas including, but not limited to, specific questions to be used on information subpoenas, and the claimant's right to notify the appropriate state or local licensing or certifying authority of an unsatisfied judgment if it arises out of the carrying on, conducting or transaction of a licensed or certified business or if such business appears to be engaged in fraudulent or illegal acts or otherwise demonstrates fraud or illegality in the carrying on, conducting or transaction of its business and a list of at least the most prominent state or local licensing or certifying authorities and a description of the business categories such licensing or certifying authorities oversee. The information shall be available in English. Large signs in English shall be posted in conspicuous locations in each small claims court clerk's office, advising the public of its availability.

(c) A defendant who wishes to file a counterclaim shall do so by filing with the clerk a statement containing such counterclaim within five days of receiving the notice of claim. At the time of such filing the defendant shall pay to the clerk a filing fee of five dollars plus the cost of mailings which are required pursuant to this subdivision. The clerk shall forthwith send notice of the counterclaim by ordinary first class mail to the claimant. If the defendant fails to file the counterclaim in accordance with the provisions of this subdivision, the defendant retains the right to file the counterclaim, however the claimant may, but shall not be required to, request and obtain adjournment of the hearing to a later date. The claimant may reply to the counterclaim but shall not be required to do so.

§ 1804. Informal and simplified procedure on small claims.

The court shall conduct hearings upon small claims in such manner as to do substantial justice between the parties according to the rules of substantive law and shall not be bound by statutory provisions or rules of practice, procedure, pleading or evidence, except statutory provisions relating to privileged communications and personal transactions or communications with a decedent or mentally ill person. An itemized bill or invoice, receipted or marked paid, or two itemized estimates for services or repairs, are admissible in evidence and are prima facie evidence of the reasonable value and necessity of such services and repairs. Disclosure shall be unavailable in small claims procedure except upon order of the court on showing of proper circumstances. In every small claims action, where the claim arises out of the conduct of the defendant's business at the hearing on the matter, the judge or arbitrator shall determine the appropriate state or local licensing or certifying authority and any business or professional association of which the defendant is a member. The provisions of this act and the rules of this court, together with the statutes and rules governing supreme court practice, shall apply to claims brought under this article so far as the same can be made applicable and are not in conflict with the provisions of this article; in case of conflict, the provisions of this article shall control.

§ 1805. Remedies available; transfer of small claims.

(a) Upon determination of a small claim, the court shall direct judgment in accordance with its findings, and, when necessary to do substantial justice between the parties, may condition the entry of judgment upon such terms as the court shall deem proper. Pursuant to section fifty-two hundred twenty-nine of the civil practice law and rules, prior to entering a judgment, the court may order the examination of or disclosure by, the defendant and restrain him to the same extent as if a restraining notice had been served upon him after judgment was entered.

(b) The court shall have power to transfer any small claim or claims to any other part of the court upon such terms as the rules may provide, and proceed to hear the same according to the usual practice and procedure applicable to other parts of the court.

(c) No counterclaim shall be permitted in a small claims action, unless the court would have had monetary jurisdiction over the counterclaim if it had been filed as a small claim. Any other claim sought to be maintained against the claimant may be filed in any court of competent jurisdiction.

(d) If the defendant appears to be engaged in repeated fraudulent or illegal acts or otherwise demonstrates persistent fraud or illegality in the carrying on, conducting or transaction of business, the court shall either advise the attorney general in relation to his authority under subdivision twelve of section sixty-three of the executive law, or shall advise the claimant to do same, but shall retain jurisdiction over the small claim.

(e) If the defendant appears to be engaged in fraudulent or illegal acts or otherwise demonstrates fraud or illegality in the carrying on, conducting or transaction of a licensed or certified business, the court shall either advise the appropriate state or local licensing or certifying authority or shall advise the claimant to do same, but shall retain jurisdiction over the small claim.

(f) The court shall have the jurisdiction defined in section three thousand one of the CPLR to make a declaratory judgment with respect to actions commenced by a party aggrieved by an arbitration award rendered pursuant to part one hundred thirty-seven of the rules of the chief administrator (22 NYCRR Part 137) in which the amount in dispute does not exceed five thousand dollars.

§ 1806. Trial by jury; how obtained; discretionary costs.

A person commencing an action upon a small claim under this article shall be deemed to have waived a trial by jury, but if said action shall be removed to a regular part of the court, the plaintiff shall have the same right to demand a trial by jury as if such action had originally been begun in such part. Any party to such action, other than the plaintiff, prior to the day upon which he is notified to appear or answer, may file with the court a demand for a trial by jury and his affidavit that there are issues of fact in the action requiring such a trial, specifying the same and stating that such trial is desired and intended in good faith. Such demand and affidavit shall be accompanied with the jury fee required by law and an undertaking in the sum of fifty dollars in such form as may be approved by the rules, payable to the other party or parties, conditioned upon the payment of any costs which may be entered against him in the said action or any appeal within thirty days after the entry thereof; or, in lieu of said undertaking, the sum of fifty dollars may be deposited with the clerk of the court and thereupon the clerk shall forthwith transmit such original papers or duly attested copies thereof as may be provided by the rules to the part of the court to which the action shall have been transferred and assigned and such part may require pleadings in such action as though it had been begun by the service of a summons. Such action may be considered a preferred cause of action. In any small claim which may have been transferred to another part of the court, the court may award costs up to twenty-five dollars to the plaintiff if he prevails.

§ 1807. Review.

A person commencing an action upon a small claim under this article shall be deemed to have waived all right to appeal, except that either party may appeal on the sole grounds that substantial justice has not been done between the parties according to the rules and principles of substantive law.

§ 1808. Judgment obtained to be res judicata in certain cases.

A judgment obtained under this article shall not otherwise be deemed an adjudication of any fact at issue or found therein in any other action or court; except that a subsequent judgment obtained in another action or court involving the same facts, issues and parties shall be reduced by the amount of a judgment awarded under this article.

§ 1809. Procedures relating to corporations, insurers and assignees.

1. No corporation, except a municipal corporation, public benefit corporation, school district or school district public library wholly or partially within the municipal corporate limit, and no assignees of any small claim shall institute an action or proceeding under this article, nor shall this article apply to any claim or cause of action brought by an insurer in its own name or in the name of its insured whether before or after payment to the insured on the policy.

2. A corporation may appear in the defense of any small claim action brought pursuant to this article by an attorney as well as by any authorized officer, director or employee of the corporation provided that the appearance by a non-lawyer on behalf of a corporation shall be deemed to constitute the requisite authority to bind the corporation in a settlement or trial. The court or arbitrator may make reasonable inquiry to determine the authority of any person who appears for the corporation in defense of a small claims court case.

§ 1810. Limitation on right to resort to small claims procedures.

If the clerk shall find that the procedures of the small claims part are sought to be utilized by a claimant for purposes of oppression or harassment, as where a claimant has previously resorted to such procedures on the same claim and has been unsuccessful after the hearing thereon, the clerk may in his discretion compel the claimant to make application to the court for leave to prosecute the claim in the small claims part. The court upon such application may inquire into the circumstances and, if it shall find that the claim has already been adjudicated, or that the claim is sought to be brought on solely for purposes of oppression or harassment and not under color of right, it may make an order denying the claimant the use of the small claims part to prosecute the claim.

§ 1811. Notice of small claims judgments and indexing of unpaid claims.

(a) Notice of judgment sent to judgment debtor shall specify that a failure to satisfy a judgment may subject the debtor to any one or combination of the following actions: 1. garnishment of wage; 2. garnishment of bank account; 3. a lien on personal property; 4. seizure and sale of real property; 5. seizure and sale of personal property, including automobiles; 6. suspension of motor vehicle license and registration, if claim is based on defendant's ownership or operation of a motor vehicle; 7. revocation, suspension, or denial of renewal of any applicable business license or permit; 8. investigation and prosecution by the attorney general for fraudulent or illegal business practices; and 9. a penalty equal to three times the amount of the unsatisfied judgment plus attorney's fees, if there are other unpaid claims.

(b) Notice of judgment sent to judgment creditor shall contain but not be limited to the following information: 1. the claimant's right to payment within thirty days following the debtor's receipt of the judgment notice; 2. the procedures for use of section eighteen hundred twelve of this article concerning the identification of assets of the judgment debtor including the use of information subpoenas, access to consumer credit reports and the role of sheriffs and marshals, and actions to collect three times the judgment award and attorney's fees if there are two other unsatisfied claims against the debtor; 3. the claimant's right to initiate actions to recover the unpaid judgment through the sale of the debtor's real property, or personal property; 4. the claimant's right to initiate actions to recover the unpaid judgment through suspension of debtor's motor vehicle license and registration, if claim is based on defendant's ownership or operation of a motor vehicle; 5. the claimant's right to notify the appropriate state or local licensing or certifying authority of an unsatisfied judgment as a basis for possible revocation, suspension, or denial of renewal of business license; and 6. a statement that upon satisfying the judgment, the judgment debtor shall present appropriate proof thereof to the court; and 7. the claimant's right to notify the attorney general if the debtor is a business and appears to be engaged in fraudulent or illegal business practices.

(c) Notice of judgment sent to each party shall include the following statement: "An appeal from this judgment must be taken no later than the earliest of the following dates: (i) thirty days after receipt in court of a copy of the judgment by the appealing party, (ii) thirty days after personal delivery of a copy of the judgment by another party to the action to the appealing party (or by the appealing party to another party), or (iii) thirty-five days after the mailing of a copy of the judgement to the appealing party by the clerk of the court or by another party to the action."

(d) All wholly or partially unsatisfied small claims court judgments shall be indexed alphabetically and chronologically under the name of the judgment debtor. Upon satisfying the judgment, the judgment debtor shall present appropriate proof to the court and the court shall indicate such in the record.

§ 1812. Enforcement of small claims judgments.

(a) The special procedures set forth in subdivision (b) hereof shall be available only where: 1. there is a recorded judgment of a small claims court; and 2. (i) the aforesaid judgment resulted from a transaction in the course of the trade or business of the judgment debtor, or arose out of a repeated course of dealing or conduct of the judgment debtor, and (ii) there are at least two other unsatisfied recorded judgments of a small claims court arising out of such trade or business or repeated course of dealing or conduct, against that judgment debtor; and 3. the judgment debtor failed to satisfy such judgment within a period of thirty days after receipt of notice of such judgment. Such notice shall be given in the same manner as provided for the service of a summons or by certified mail, return receipt requested, and shall contain a statement that such judgment exists, that at least two other unsatisfied recorded judgments exist, and that failure to pay such judgment may be the basis for an action, for treble the amount of such unsatisfied judgment, pursuant to this section.

(b) Where each of the elements of subdivision (a) of this section are present the judgment creditor shall be entitled to commence an action against said judgment debtor for treble the amount of such unsatisfied judgment, together with reasonable counsel fees, and the costs and disbursements of such action, provided, however, that in any such action it shall be a defense that the judgment debtor did not have resources to satisfy such judgment within a period of thirty days after receipt of notice of such judgment. The failure to pay a judgment obtained in an action pursuant to this section shall not be the basis for another such action pursuant to this section.

(c) Where the judgment is obtained in an action pursuant to subdivision (b), and arises from a business of the defendant, the court shall, in addition to its responsibilities under this article, advise the attorney general in relation to his authority under subdivision twelve of section sixty-three of the executive law, and if such judgment arises from a certified or licensed business of the defendant, advise the state or local licensing or certifying authority.

(d) Where a judgment has been entered in a small claims court and remains unsatisfied, the small claims clerk shall, upon request, issue information subpoenas, at nominal cost, for the judgment creditor and provide the creditor with assistance on their preparation and use. The court shall have the same power as the supreme court to punish a contempt of court committed with respect to an information subpoena.

§ 1813. Duty to pay judgments.

(a) Any person, partnership, firm or corporation which is sued in a small claims court for any cause of action arising out of its business activities, shall pay any judgment rendered against it in its true name or in any name in which it conducts business. "True name" includes the legal name of a natural person and the name under which a partnership, firm or corporation is licensed, registered, incorporated or otherwise authorized to do business. "Conducting business" as used in this section shall include, but not be limited to, maintaining signs at business premises or on business vehicles; advertising; entering into contracts; and printing or using sales slips, checks, invoices or receipts. Whenever a judgment has been rendered against a person, partnership, firm or corporation in other than its true name and the judgment has remained unpaid for thirty-five days after receipt by the judgment debtor of notice of its entry, the aggrieved judgment creditor shall be entitled to commence an action in small claims court against such judgment debtor, notwithstanding the jurisdictional limit of the court, for the sum of the original judgment, costs, reasonable attorney's fees, and one hundred dollars.

(b) Whenever a judgment which relates to activities for which a license is required has been rendered against a business which is licensed by a state or local licensing authority and which remains unpaid for thirty-five days after receipt by the judgment debtor of notice of its entry and the judgment has not been stayed or appealed, the state or local licensing authority shall consider such failure to pay, if deliberate or part of a pattern of similar conduct indicating recklessness, as a basis for the revocation, suspension, conditioning or refusal to grant or renew such license. Nothing herein shall be construed to preempt an authority's existing policy if it is more restrictive.

(c) The clerk shall attach to the notice of suit required under this article a notice of the duty imposed by this section.

§ 1814. Designation of defendant; amendment procedure.

(a) A party who is ignorant, in whole or in part, of the true name of a person, partnership, firm or corporation which may properly be made a party defendant, may proceed against such defendant in any name used by the person, partnership, firm or corporation in conducting business, as defined in subdivision (a) of section eighteen hundred thirteen of this article.

(b) If the true name of the defendant becomes known at any time prior to the hearing on the merits, such information shall be brought to the attention of the clerk, who shall immediately amend all prior proceedings and papers. The clerk shall send an amended notice to the defendant, without payment of additional fees by the plaintiff, and all subsequent proceedings and papers shall be amended accordingly.

(c) In every action in the small claims part, at the hearing on the merits, the judge or arbitrator shall determine the defendant's true name. The clerk shall amend all prior proceedings and papers to conform to such determination, and all subsequent proceedings and papers shall be amended accordingly.

(d) A party against whom a judgment has been entered pursuant to this article, in any proceeding under section five thousand fifteen of the civil practice law and rules for relief from such judgment, shall, disclose its true name; any and all names in which it is conducting business; and any and all names in which it was conducting business at the time of the transaction or occurrence on which such judgment is based. All subsequent proceedings and papers shall be amended to conform to such disclosure.

§ 1815. Appearance by non-attorney representatives.

The court may permit, upon the request of a party, that a non-attorney representative, who is related by consanguinity or affinity to such party, be allowed to appear on behalf of such party when the court finds that due to the age, mental or physical capacity or other disability of such party that it is in the interests of justice to permit such representation. No person acting as a non-attorney representative shall be permitted to charge a fee or be allowed to accept any form of remuneration for such services.

Appendix D

Uniform City Court Act
Article 18 - Small Claims

§ 1801. Small claims defined.

The term "small claim" or "small claims" as used in this act shall mean and include any cause of action for money only not in excess of five thousand dollars exclusive of interest and costs, or any action commenced by a party aggrieved by an arbitration award rendered pursuant to part one hundred thirty-seven of the rules of the chief administrator of the courts (22 NYCRR Part 137) in which the amount in dispute does not exceed $5,000, provided that the defendant either resides, or has an office for the transaction of business or a regular employment, within the county.

§ 1802. Parts for the determination of small claims established.

The chief administrator shall assign the times and places for holding, and the judges who shall hold, one or more parts of the court for the hearing of small claims as herein defined, and the rules may regulate the practice and procedure controlling the determination of such claims and prescribe and furnish the forms for instituting the same. There shall be at least one evening session of each part every month for the hearing of small claims, provided however, that the chief administrator may provide for exemption from this requirement where there exists no demonstrated need for evening sessions. Such practice, procedure and forms shall differ from the practice, procedure and forms used in the court for other than small claims, notwithstanding any provision of law to the contrary. They shall constitute a simple, informal and inexpensive procedure for the prompt determination of such claims in accordance with the rules and principles of substantive law. The procedure established pursuant to this article shall not be exclusive of but shall be alternative to the procedure now or hereafter established with respect to actions commenced in the court by the service of a summons. No rule to be enacted pursuant to this article shall dispense with or interfere with the taking of stenographic minutes of any hearing of any small claim hereunder, except that in cities with a population of fifty thousand or less hearings may be recorded mechanically.

§ 1803. Commencement of action upon small claims.

(a) Small claims shall be commenced upon the payment by the claimant of a filing fee of fifteen dollars for claims in the amount of one thousand dollars or less and twenty dollars for claims in the amount of more than one thousand dollars, without the service of a summons and, except by special order of the court, without the service of any pleading other than a statement of his cause of action by the claimant or someone in his behalf to the clerk, who shall reduce the same to a concise, written form and record it in a docket kept especially for such purpose. Such procedure shall provide for the sending of notice of such claim by ordinary first class mail and certified mail with return receipt requested to the party complained against at his residence, if he resides within the county, and his residence is known to the claimant, or at his office or place of regular employment within the county if he does not reside therein or his residence within the county is not known to the claimant. If, after the expiration of twenty-one days, such ordinary first class mailing has not been returned as undeliverable, the party complained against shall be presumed to have received notice of such claim. Such notice shall include a clear description of the procedure for filing a counterclaim, pursuant to subdivision (c) of this section. Such procedure shall further provide for an early hearing upon and determination of such claim. No filing fee, however, shall be demanded or received on small claims of employees who shall comply with § 1912 of this act which is hereby made applicable, except that necessary mailing costs shall be paid.

(b) The clerk shall furnish every claimant, upon commencement of the action, with information written in clear and coherent language which shall be prescribed and furnished by the office of court administration, concerning the small claims court. Such information shall include, but not be limited to, an explanation of the following terms and procedures; adjournments, counterclaims, jury trial requests, subpoenas, arbitration, collection methods and fees, the responsibility of the judgment creditor to collect data on the judgment debtor's assets, the ability of the court prior to entering judgment to order examination of or disclosure by, the defendant and restrain him, the utilization of section eighteen hundred twelve of this article concerning treble damage awards and information subpoenas including, but not limited to, specific questions to be used on information subpoenas, and the claimant's right to notify the appropriate state or local licensing or certifying authority of an unsatisfied judgment if it arises out of the carrying on, conducting or transaction of a licensed or certified business or if such business appears to be engaged in fraudulent or illegal acts or otherwise demonstrates fraud or illegality in the carrying on, conducting or transaction of its business and a list of at least the most prominent state or local licensing or certifying authorities and a description of the business categories such licensing or certifying authorities oversee. The information shall be available in English. Large signs in English shall be posted in conspicuous locations in each small claims court clerk's office, advising the public of its availability.

(c) A defendant who wishes to file a counterclaim shall do so by filing with the clerk a statement containing such counterclaim within five days of receiving the notice of claim. At the time of such filing the defendant shall pay to the clerk a filing fee of five dollars plus the cost of mailings which are required pursuant to this subdivision. The clerk shall forthwith send notice of the counterclaim by ordinary first class mail to the claimant. If the defendant fails to file the counterclaim in accordance with the provisions of this subdivision, the defendant retains the right to file the counterclaim, however the claimant may, but shall not be required to, request and obtain adjournment of the hearing to a later date. The claimant may reply to the counterclaim but shall not be required to do so.

§ 1804. Informal and simplified procedure on small claims.

The court shall conduct hearings upon small claims in such manner as to do substantial justice between the parties according to the rules of substantive law and shall not be bound by statutory provisions or rules of practice, procedure, pleading or evidence, except statutory provisions relating to privileged communications and personal transactions or communications with a decedent or mentally ill person. An itemized bill or invoice, receipted or marked paid, or two itemized estimates for services or repairs, are admissible in evidence and are prima facie evidence of the reasonable value and necessity of such services and repairs. Disclosure shall be unavailable in small claims procedure except upon order of the court on showing of proper circumstances. In every small claims action, where the claim arises out of the conduct of the defendant's business at the hearing on the matter, the judge or arbitrator shall determine the appropriate state or local licensing or certifying authority and any business or professional association of which the defendant is a member. The provisions of this act and the rules of this court, together with the statutes and rules governing supreme court practice, shall apply to claims brought under this article so far as the same can be made applicable and are not in conflict with the provisions of this article; in case of conflict, the provisions of this article shall control.

§ 1805. Remedies available; transfer of small claims.

(a) Upon determination of a small claim, the court shall direct judgment in accordance with its findings, and, when necessary to do substantial justice between the parties, may condition the entry of judgment upon such terms as the court shall deem proper. Pursuant to section fifty-two hundred twenty-nine of the civil practice law and rules, prior to entering a judgment, the court may order the examination of or disclosure by, the defendant and restrain him to the same extent as if a restraining notice had been served upon him after judgment was entered.

(b) The court shall have power to transfer any small claim or claims to any other part of the court upon such terms as the rules may provide, and proceed to hear the same according to the usual practice and procedure applicable to other parts of the court.

(c) No counterclaim shall be permitted in a small claims action, unless the court would have had monetary jurisdiction over the counterclaim if it had been filed as a small claim. Any other claim sought to be maintained against the claimant may be filed in any court of competent jurisdiction.

(d) If the defendant appears to be engaged in repeated fraudulent or illegal acts or otherwise demonstrates persistent fraud or illegality in the carrying on, conducting or transaction of business, the court shall either advise the attorney general in relation to his authority under subdivision twelve of section sixty-three of the executive law, or shall advise the claimant to do same, but shall retain jurisdiction over the small claim.

(e) If the defendant appears to be engaged in fraudulent or illegal acts or otherwise demonstrates fraud or illegality in the carrying on, conducting or transaction of a licensed or certified business, the court shall either advise the appropriate state or local licensing or certifying authority or shall advise the claimant to do same, but shall retain jurisdiction over the small claim.

(f) The court shall have the jurisdiction defined in section three thousand one of the CPLR to make a declaratory judgment with respect to actions commenced by a party aggrieved by an arbitration award rendered pursuant to part one hundred thirty-seven of the rules of the chief administrator (22 NYCRR Part 137) in which the amount in dispute does not exceed $5,000.

§ 1806. Trial by jury; how obtained; discretionary costs.

A person commencing an action upon a small claim under this article shall be deemed to have waived a trial by jury, but if said action shall be removed to a regular part of the court, the plaintiff shall have the same right to demand a trial by jury as if such action had originally been begun in such part. Any party to such action, other than the plaintiff, prior to the day upon which he is notified to appear or answer, may file with the court a demand for a trial by jury and his affidavit that there are issues of fact in the action requiring such a trial, specifying the same and stating that such trial is desired and intended in good faith. Such demand and affidavit shall be accompanied with the jury fee required by law and an undertaking in the sum of fifty dollars in such form as may be approved by the rules, payable to the other party or parties, conditioned upon the payment of any costs which may be entered against him in the said action or any appeal within thirty days after the entry thereof; or, in lieu of said undertaking, the sum of fifty dollars may be deposited with the clerk of the court and thereupon the clerk shall forthwith transmit such original papers or duly attested copies thereof as may be provided by the rules to the part of the court to which the action shall have been transferred and assigned and such part may require pleadings in such action as though it had been begun by the service of a summons. Such action may be considered a preferred cause of action. In any small claim which may have been transferred to another part of the court, the court may award costs up to twenty-five dollars to the plaintiff if he prevails.

§ 1807. Review.

A person commencing an action upon a small claim under this article shall be deemed to have waived all right to appeal, except that either party may appeal on the sole grounds that substantial justice has not been done between the parties according to the rules and principles of substantive law.

§ 1808. Judgment obtained to be res judicata in certain cases.

A judgment obtained under this article shall not otherwise be deemed an adjudication of any fact at issue or found therein in any other action or court; except that a subsequent judgment obtained in another action or court involving the same facts, issues and parties shall be reduced by the amount of a judgment awarded under this article.

§ 1809. Procedures relating to corporations, associations, insurers and assignees.

1. No corporation, except a municipal corporation, public benefit corporation, school district or school district public library wholly or partially within the municipal corporate limit, no partnership, or association and no assignee of any small claim shall institute an action or proceeding under this article, nor shall this article apply to any claim or cause of action brought by an insurer in its own name or in the name of its insured whether before or after payment to the insured on the policy.

2. A corporation may appear in the defense of any small claim action brought pursuant to this article by an attorney as well as by any authorized officer, director or employee of the corporation provided that the appearance by a non-lawyer on behalf of a corporation shall be deemed to constitute the

requisite authority to bind the corporation in a settlement or trial. The court or arbitrator may make reasonable inquiry to determine the authority of any person who appears for the corporation in defense of a small claims court case.

§ 1810. Limitation on right to resort to small claims procedures.

If the clerk shall find that the procedures of the small claims part are sought to be utilized by a claimant for purposes of oppression or harassment, as where a claimant has previously resorted to such procedures on the same claim and has been unsuccessful after the hearing thereon, the clerk may in his discretion compel the claimant to make application to the court for leave to prosecute the claim in the small claims part. The court upon such application may inquire into the circumstances and, if it shall find that the claim has already been adjudicated, or that the claim is sought to be brought on solely for purposes of oppression or harassment and not under color of right, it may make an order denying the claimant the use of the small claims part to prosecute the claim.

§ 1811. Notice of small claims judgments and indexing of unpaid claims.

(a) Notice of judgment sent to judgment debtor shall specify that a failure to satisfy a judgment may subject the debtor to any one or combination of the following actions: 1. garnishment of wage; 2. garnishment of bank account; 3. a lien on personal property; 4. seizure and sale of real property; 5. seizure and sale of personal property, including automobiles; 6. suspension of motor vehicle license and registration, if claim is based on defendant's ownership or operation of a motor vehicle; 7. revocation, suspension, or denial of renewal of any applicable business license or permit; 8. investigation and prosecution by the attorney general for fraudulent or illegal business practices; and 9. a penalty equal to three times the amount of the unsatisfied judgment plus attorney's fees, if there are other unpaid claims. (b) Notice of judgment sent to judgment creditor shall contain but not be limited to the following information: 1. the claimant's right to payment within thirty days following the debtor's receipt of the judgment notice; 2. the procedures for use of section eighteen hundred twelve of this article concerning the identification of assets of the judgment debtor including the use of information subpoenas, access to consumer credit reports and the role of sheriffs and marshals, and actions to collect three times the judgment award and attorney's fees if there are two other unsatisfied claims against the debtor; 3. the claimant's right to initiate actions to recover the unpaid judgment through the sale of the debtor's real property, or personal property; 4. the claimant's right to initiate actions to recover the unpaid judgment through suspension of debtor's motor vehicle license and registration, if claim is based on defendant's ownership or operation of a motor vehicle; 5. the claimant's right to notify the appropriate state or local licensing or certifying authority of an unsatisfied judgment as a basis for possible revocation, suspension, or denial of renewal of business license; and 6. a statement that upon satisfying the judgment, the judgment debtor shall present appropriate proof thereof to the court; and 7. the claimant's right to notify the attorney general if the debtor is a business and appears to be engaged in fraudulent or illegal business practices. (c) Notice of judgment sent to each party shall include the following statement: "An appeal from this judgment must be taken no later than the earliest of the following dates: (i) thirty days after receipt in court of a copy of the judgment by the appealing party, (ii) thirty days after personal delivery of a copy of the judgment by another party to the action to the appealing party (or by the appealing party to another party), or (iii) thirty-five days after the mailing of a copy of the judgment to the appealing party by the clerk of the court or by another party to the action." (d) All wholly or partially unsatisfied small claims court judgments shall be indexed alphabetically and chronologically under the name of the judgment debtor. Upon satisfying the judgment, the judgment debtor shall present appropriate proof to the court and the court shall indicate such in the records.

§ 1812. Enforcement of small claims judgments.

(a) The special procedures set forth in subdivision (b) hereof shall be available only where: 1. there is a recorded judgment of a small claims court; and 2. (i) the aforesaid judgment resulted from a transaction in the course of the trade or business of the judgment debtor, or arose out of a repeated course of dealing or conduct of the judgment debtor, and (ii) there are at least two other unsatisfied recorded judgments of a small claims court arising out of such trade or business or repeated course of dealing or conduct, against that judgment debtor; and 3. the judgment debtor failed to satisfy such judgment within a period of thirty days after receipt of notice of such judgment. Such notice shall be given in the same manner as provided for the service of a summons or by certified mail, return receipt requested, and shall contain a statement that such judgment exists, that at least two other unsatisfied recorded judgments exist, and that failure to pay such judgment may be the basis for an action, for treble the amount of such unsatisfied judgment, pursuant to this section.

(b) Where each of the elements of subdivision (a) of this section are present the judgment creditor shall be entitled to commence an action against said judgment debtor for treble the amount of such unsatisfied judgment, together with reasonable counsel fees, and the costs and disbursements of such action, provided, however, that in any such action it shall be a defense that the judgment debtor did not have resources to satisfy such judgment within a period of thirty days after receipt of notice of such judgment. The failure to pay a judgment obtained in an action pursuant to this section shall not be the basis for another such action pursuant to this section.

(c) Where the judgment is obtained in an action pursuant to subdivision (b), and arises from a business of the defendant, the court shall, in addition to its responsibilities under this article, advise the attorney general in relation to his authority under subdivision twelve of section sixty-three of the executive law, and if such judgment arises from a certified or licensed business of the defendant, advise the state or local licensing or certifying authority.

(d) Where a judgment has been entered in a small claims court and remains unsatisfied, the small claims clerk shall, upon request, issue information subpoenas, at nominal cost, for the judgment creditor and provide the creditor with assistance on their preparation and use. The court shall have the same power as the supreme court to punish a contempt of court committed with respect to an information subpoena.

§ 1813. Duty to pay judgments.

(a) Any person, partnership, firm or corporation which is sued in a small claims court for any cause of action arising out of its business activities, shall pay any judgment rendered against it in its true name or in any name in which it conducts business. "True name" includes the legal name of a natural person and the name under which a partnership, firm or corporation is licensed, registered, incorporated or otherwise authorized to do business. "Conducting business" as used in this section shall include, but not be limited to, maintaining signs at business premises or on business vehicles; advertising; entering into contracts; and printing or using sales slips, checks, invoices or receipts. Whenever a judgment has been rendered against a person, partnership, firm or corporation in other than its true name and the judgment has remained unpaid for thirty-five days after receipt by the judgment debtor of notice of its entry, the aggrieved judgment creditor shall be entitled to commence an action in small claims court against such judgment debtor, notwithstanding the jurisdictional limit of the court, for the sum of the original judgment, costs, reasonable attorney's fees, and one hundred dollars.

(b) Whenever a judgment which relates to activities for which a license is required has been rendered against a business which is licensed by a state or local licensing authority and which remains unpaid for thirty-five days after receipt by the judgment debtor of notice of its entry and the judgment has not been stayed or appealed, the state or local licensing authority shall consider such failure to pay, if deliberate or part of a pattern of similar conduct indicating recklessness, as a basis for the revocation, suspension, conditioning or refusal to grant or renew such license. Nothing herein shall be construed to preempt an authority's existing policy if it is more restrictive.

(c) The clerk shall attach to the notice of suit required under this article a notice of the duty imposed by this section.

§ 1814. Designation of defendant; amendment procedure.

(a) A party who is ignorant, in whole or in part, of the true name of a person, partnership, firm or corporation which may properly be made a party defendant, may proceed against such defendant in any name used by the person, partnership, firm or corporation in conducting business, as defined in subdivision (a) of section eighteen hundred thirteen of this article.

(b) If the true name of the defendant becomes known at any time prior to the hearing on the merits, such information shall be brought to the attention of the clerk, who shall immediately amend all prior proceedings and papers. The clerk shall send an amended notice to the defendant, without payment of additional fees by the plaintiff, and all subsequent proceedings and papers shall be amended accordingly.

(c) In every action in the small claims part, at the hearing on the merits, the judge or arbitrator shall determine the defendant's true name. The clerk shall amend all prior proceedings and papers to conform to such determination, and all subsequent proceedings and papers shall be amended accordingly.

(d) A party against whom a judgment has been entered pursuant to this article, in any proceeding under section five thousand fifteen of the civil practice law and rules for relief from such judgment, shall, disclose its true name; any and all names in which it is conducting business; and any and all names in which it was conducting business at the time of the transaction or occurrence on which such judgment is based. All subsequent proceedings and papers shall be amended to conform to such disclosure.

§ 1815. Appearance by non-attorney representatives.

The court may permit, upon the request of a party, that a non-attorney representative, who is related by consanguinity or affinity to such party, be allowed to appear on behalf of such party when the court finds that due to the age, mental or physical capacity or other disability of such party that it is in the interests of justice to permit such representation. No person acting as a non-attorney representative shall be permitted to charge a fee or be allowed to accept any form of remuneration for such services.

Appendix E

Uniform Justice Court Act
Article 18 - Small Claims

§ 1801. Small claims defined.

The term "small claim" or "small claims" as used in this act shall mean and include any cause of action for money only not in excess of three thousand dollars exclusive of interest and costs, provided that the defendant either resides, or has an office for the transaction of business or a regular employment, within the municipality where the court is located. However, where a judge of the county court, pursuant to subdivision (g) of section three hundred twenty-five of the civil practice law and rules, transfers a small claim from the town or village court having jurisdiction over the matter to another town or village court within the same county, the court to which it is transferred shall have jurisdiction to determine the claim.

§ 1802. Parts for the determination of small claims established.

The chief administrator shall assign the times and places for holding, and the judges who shall hold, one or more parts of the court for the hearing of small claims as herein defined, and the rules may regulate the practice and procedure controlling the determination of such claims and prescribe and furnish the forms for instituting the same. There shall be at least one evening session of each part every month for the hearing of small claims, provided however, that the chief administrator may provide for exemption from this requirement where there exists no demonstrated need for evening sessions. Such practice, procedure and forms shall differ from the practice, procedure and forms used in the court for other than small claims, notwithstanding any provision of law to the contrary. They shall constitute a simple, informal and inexpensive procedure for the prompt determination of such claims in accordance with the rules and principles of substantive law. The procedure established pursuant to this article shall not be exclusive of but shall be alternative to this procedure now or hereafter established with respect to actions commenced in the court by the service of a summons. No rule to be enacted pursuant to this article shall dispense with or interfere with the taking of stenographic minutes of any hearing of any small claim hereunder.

§ 1803. Commencement of action upon small claims.

(a) Small claims shall be commenced upon the payment by the claimant of a filing fee of ten dollars for claims in the amount of one thousand dollars or less and fifteen dollars for claims in the amount of more than one thousand dollars, without the service of a summons and, except by special order of the court, without the service of any pleading other than a statement of his cause of action by the claimant or someone in his behalf to the clerk, who shall reduce the same to a concise, written form and record it in a filing system maintained especially for such purpose. Such procedure shall provide for the sending of notice of such claim by ordinary first class mail and certified mail with return receipt requested to the party complained against at his residence, if he resides within the county and his residence is known to the claimant, or at his office or place of regular employment within the municipality if he does not reside within the county or his residence within the county is not known to the claimant. If, after the expiration of twenty-one days, such ordinary first class mailing has not been returned as undeliverable, the party complained against shall be presumed to have received notice of such claim. Such notice shall include a clear description of the procedure for filing a counterclaim, pursuant to subdivision (c) of this section. Such procedure shall further provide for an early hearing upon and determination of such claim. No filing fee, however, shall be demanded or received on small claims of employees who shall comply with section nineteen hundred twelve of this act which is hereby made applicable, except that necessary mailing costs shall be paid.

(b) The clerk shall furnish every claimant, upon commencement of the action, with information written in clear and coherent language which shall be prescribed and furnished by the office of court administration, concerning the small claims court. Such information shall include, but not be limited to, an explanation of the following terms and procedures; adjournments, counterclaims, jury trial requests, subpoenas, arbitration, collection methods and fees, the responsibility of the judgment creditor to collect data on the judgment debtor's assets, the ability of the court prior to entering judgment to order examination of or disclosure by, the defendant and restrain him, the utilization of section eighteen hundred twelve of this article concerning treble damage awards and information subpoenas including, but not limited to, specific questions to be used on information subpoenas, and the claimant's right to notify the appropriate state or local licensing or certifying authority of an unsatisfied judgment if it arises out of the carrying on, conducting or transaction of a licensed or certified business or if such business appears to be engaged in fraudulent or illegal acts or otherwise demonstrates fraud or illegality in the carrying on, conducting or transaction of its business. The information shall be available in English. Large signs in English shall be posted in conspicuous locations in each small claims court clerk's office, advising the public of its availability.

(c) A defendant who wishes to file a counterclaim shall do so by filing with the clerk a statement containing such counterclaim within five days of receiving the notice of claim. At the time of such filing the defendant shall pay to the clerk a filing fee of three dollars plus the cost of mailings which are required pursuant to this subdivision. The clerk shall forthwith send notice of the counterclaim by ordinary first class mail to the claimant. If the defendant fails to file the counterclaim in accordance with the provisions of this subdivision, the defendant retains the right to file the counterclaim, however the claimant may, but shall not be required to, request and obtain adjournment of the hearing to a later date. The claimant may reply to the counterclaim but shall not be required to do so.

§ 1804. Informal and simplified procedure on small claims.

The court shall conduct hearings upon small claims in such manner as to do substantial justice between the parties according to the rules of substantive law and shall not be bound by statutory provisions or rules of practice, procedure, pleading or evidence, except statutory provisions relating to privileged communications and personal transactions or communications with a decedent or mentally ill person. An itemized bill or invoice, receipted or marked paid, or two itemized estimates for services or repairs, are admissible in evidence and are prima facie evidence of the reasonable value and necessity of such services and repairs. Disclosure shall be unavailable in small claims procedure except upon order of the court on showing of proper circumstances. In every small claims action, where the claim arises out of the conduct of the defendant's business at the hearing on the matter, the judge or arbitrator shall determine the appropriate state or local licensing or certifying authority and any business or professional association of which the defendant is a member. The provisions of this act and the rules of this court, together with the statutes and rules governing supreme court practice, shall apply to claims brought under this article so far as the same can be made applicable and are not in conflict with the provisions of this article; in case of conflict, the provisions of this article shall control.

§ 1805. Remedies available; transfer of small claims.

(a) Upon determination of a small claim, the court shall direct judgment in accordance with its findings, and, when necessary to do substantial justice between the parties, may condition the entry of judgment upon such terms as the court shall deem proper. Pursuant to section fifty-two hundred twenty-nine of the civil practice law and rules, prior to entering a judgment, the court may order the examination of or disclosure by, the defendant and restrain him to the same extent as if a restraining notice had been served upon him after judgment was entered.

(b) The court shall have power to transfer any small claim or claims to any other part of the court upon such terms as the rules may provide, and proceed to hear the same according to the usual practice and procedure applicable to other parts of the court.

(c) No counterclaim shall be permitted in a small claims action, unless the court would have had monetary jurisdiction over the counterclaim if it had been filed as a small claim. Any other claim sought to be maintained against the claimant may be filed in any court of competent jurisdiction.

(d) If the defendant appears to be engaged in repeated fraudulent or illegal acts or otherwise demonstrates persistent fraud or illegality in the carrying on, conducting or transaction of business, the court shall either advise the attorney general in relation to his authority under subdivision twelve of section sixty-three of the executive law, or shall advise the claimant to do same, but shall retain jurisdiction over the small claim.

(e) If the defendant appears to be engaged in fraudulent or illegal acts or otherwise demonstrates fraud or illegality in the carrying on, conducting or transaction of a licensed or certified business, the court shall either advise the appropriate state or local licensing or certifying authority or shall advise the claimant to do same, but shall retain jurisdiction over the small claim.

§ 1806. Trial by jury; how obtained; discretionary costs.

A person commencing an action upon a small claim under this article shall be deemed to have waived a trial by jury, but if said action shall be removed to a regular part of the court, the plaintiff shall have the same right to demand a trial by jury as if such action had originally been begun in such part. Any party to such action, other than the plaintiff, prior to the day upon which he is notified to appear or answer, may file with the court a demand for a trial by jury and his affidavit that there are issues of fact in the action requiring such a trial, specifying the same and stating that such trial is desired and intended in good faith. Such demand and affidavit shall be accompanied with the jury fee required by law and an undertaking in the sum of fifty dollars in such form as may be approved by the rules, payable to the other parts or parties, conditioned upon the payment of any costs which may be entered against him in the said action or any appeal within thirty days after the entry thereof; or, in lieu of said undertaking, the sum of fifty dollars may be deposited with the clerk of the court and thereupon the clerk shall forthwith transmit such original papers or duly attested copies thereof as may be provided by the rules to the part of the court to which the action shall have been transferred and assigned and such part may require pleadings in such action as though it had been begun by the service of a summons. Such action may be considered a preferred cause of action. In any small claim which may have been transferred to another part of the court, the court may award costs up to twenty-five dollars to the plaintiff if he prevails.

§ 1807. Review.

A person commencing an action upon a small claim under this article shall be deemed to have waived all right to appeal, except that either party may appeal on the sole grounds that substantial justice has not been done between the parties according to the rules and principles of substantive law.

§ 1808. Judgment obtained to be res judicata in certain cases.

A judgment obtained under this article shall not otherwise be deemed an adjudication of any fact at issue or found therein in any other action or court; except that a subsequent judgment obtained in another action or court involving the same facts, issues and parties shall be reduced by the amount of a judgment awarded under this article.

§ 1809. Procedures relating to corporations, associations, insurers and assignees.

1. No corporation, except a municipal corporation, public benefit corporation, school district or school district public library wholly or partially within the municipal corporate limit, no partnership, or association and no assignee of any small claim shall institute an action or proceeding under this article, nor shall this article apply to any claim or cause of action brought by an insurer in its own name or in the name of its insured whether before or after payment to the insured on the policy.

2. A corporation may appear in the defense of any small claim action brought pursuant to this article by an attorney as well as by any authorized officer, director or employee of the corporation provided that the appearance by a non-lawyer on behalf of a corporation shall be deemed to constitute the requisite authority to bind the corporation in a settlement or trial. The court or arbitrator may make reasonable inquiry to determine the authority of any person who appears for the corporation in defense of a small claims court case.

§ 1810. Limitation on right to resort to small claims procedures.

If the clerk shall find that the procedures of the small claims part are sought to be utilized by a claimant for purposes of oppression or harassment, as where a claimant has previously resorted to such procedures on the same claim and has been unsuccessful after the hearing thereon, the clerk may in his discretion compel the claimant to make application to the court for leave to prosecute the claim in the small claims part. The court upon such application may inquire into the circumstances and, if it shall find that the claim has already been adjudicated, or that the claim is sought to be brought on solely for purposes of oppression or harassment and not under color of right, it may make an order denying the claimant the use of the small claims part to prosecute the claim.

§ 1811. Notice of small claims judgments and indexing of unpaid claims.

(a) Notice of judgment sent to judgment debtor shall specify that a failure to satisfy a judgment may subject the debtor to any one or combination of the following actions: 1. garnishment of wage; 2. garnishment of bank account; 3. a lien on personal property; 4. seizure and sale of real property; 5. seizure and sale of personal property, including automobiles; 6. suspension of motor vehicle license and registration, if claim is based on defendant's ownership or operation of a motor vehicle; 7. revocation, suspension, or denial of renewal of any applicable business license or permit; 8. investigation and prosecution by the attorney general for fraudulent or illegal business practices; and 9. a penalty equal to three times the amount of the unsatisfied judgment plus attorney's fees, if there are other unpaid claims.

(b) Notice of judgment sent to judgment creditor shall contain but not be limited to the following information: 1. the claimant's right to payment within thirty days following the debtor's receipt of the judgment notice; 2. the procedures for use of section eighteen hundred twelve of this article concerning the identification of assets of the judgment debtor including the use of information subpoenas, access to consumer credit reports and the role of sheriffs and marshals, and actions to collect three times the judgment award and attorney's fees if there are two other unsatisfied claims against the debtor; 3. the claimant's right to initiate actions to recover the unpaid judgment through the sale of the debtor's real property, or personal property; 4. the claimant's right to initiate actions to recover the unpaid judgment through suspension of debtor's motor vehicle license and registration, if claim is based on defendant's ownership or operation of a motor vehicle; 5. the claimant's right to notify the appropriate state or local licensing or certifying authority of an unsatisfied judgment as a basis for possible revocation, suspension, or denial of renewal of business license; and 6. a statement that upon satisfying the judgment, the judgment debtor shall present appropriate proof thereof to the court; and 7. the claimant's right to notify the attorney general if the debtor is a business and appears to be engaged in fraudulent or illegal business practices.

(c) Notice of judgment sent to each party shall include the following statement: "An appeal from this judgment must be taken no later than the earliest of the following dates: (i) thirty days after receipt in court of a copy of the judgment by the appealing party, (ii) thirty days after personal delivery of a copy of the judgment by another party to the action to the appealing party (or by the appealing party to another party), or (iii) thirty-five days after the mailing of a copy of the judgment to the appealing party by the clerk of the court or by another party to the action."

(d) All wholly or partially unsatisfied small claims court judgments shall be indexed alphabetically and chronologically under the name of the judgment debtor. Upon satisfying the judgment, the judgment debtor shall present appropriate proof to the court and the court shall indicate such in the record.

§ 1812. Enforcement of small claims judgments.

(a) The special procedures set forth in subdivision (b) hereof shall be available only where: 1. there is a recorded judgment of a small claims court; and 2. (i) the aforesaid judgment resulted from a transaction in the course of the trade or business of the judgment debtor, or arose out of a repeated course of dealing or conduct of the judgment debtor, and (ii) there are at least two other unsatisfied recorded judgments of a small claims court arising out of such trade or business or repeated course of dealing or conduct, against that judgment debtor; and 3. the judgment debtor failed to satisfy such judgment within a period of thirty days after receipt of notice of such judgment. Such notice shall be given in the same manner as provided for the service of a summons or by certified mail, return receipt requested, and shall contain a statement that such judgment exists, that at least two other unsatisfied recorded judgments exist, and that failure to pay such judgment may be the basis for an action, for treble the amount of such unsatisfied judgment, pursuant to this section.

(b) Where each of the elements of subdivision (a) of this section are present the judgment creditor shall be entitled to commence an action against said judgment debtor for treble the amount of such unsatisfied judgment, together with reasonable counsel fees, and the costs and disbursements of such action, provided, however, that in any such action it shall be a defense that the judgment debtor did not have resources to satisfy such judgment within a period of thirty days after receipt of notice of such judgment. The failure to pay a judgment obtained in an action pursuant to this section shall not be the basis for another such action pursuant to this section.

(c) Where the judgment is obtained in an action pursuant to subdivision (b), and arises from a business of the defendant, the court shall, in addition to its responsibilities under this article, advise the attorney general in relation to his authority under subdivision twelve of section sixty-three of the executive law, and if such judgment arises from a certified or licensed business of the defendant, advise the state or local licensing or certifying authority.

(d) Where a judgment has been entered in a small claims court and remains unsatisfied, the small claims clerk shall, upon request, issue information subpoenas, at nominal cost, for the judgment creditor and provide the creditor with assistance on their preparation and use. The court shall have the same power as the supreme court to punish a contempt of court committed with respect to an information subpoena.

§ 1813. Duty to pay judgments.

(a) Any person, partnership, firm or corporation which is sued in a small claims court for any cause of action arising out of its business activities, shall pay any judgment rendered against it in its true name or in any name in which it conducts business. "True name" includes the legal name of a natural person and the name under which a partnership, firm or corporation is licensed, registered, incorporated or otherwise authorized to do business. "Conducting business" as used in this section shall include, but not be limited to, maintaining signs at business premises or on business vehicles; advertising; entering into contracts; and printing or using sales slips, checks, invoices or receipts. Whenever a judgment has been rendered against a person, partnership, firm or corporation in other than its true name and the judgment has remained unpaid for thirty-five days after receipt by the judgment debtor of notice of its entry, the aggrieved judgment creditor shall be entitled to commence an action in small claims court against such judgment debtor, notwithstanding the jurisdictional limit of the court, for the sum of the original judgment, costs, reasonable attorney's fees, and one hundred dollars.

(b) Whenever a judgment which relates to activities for which a license is required has been rendered against a business which is licensed by a state or local licensing authority and which remains unpaid for thirty-five days after receipt by the judgment debtor of notice of its entry and the judgment has not been stayed or appealed, the state or local licensing authority shall consider such failure to pay, if deliberate or part of a pattern of similar conduct indicating recklessness, as a basis for the revocation, suspension, conditioning or refusal to grant or renew such license. Nothing herein shall be construed to preempt an authority's existing policy if it is more restrictive.

(c) The clerk shall attach to the notice of suit required under this article a notice of the duty imposed by this section.

§ 1814. Designation of defendant; amendment procedure.

(a) A party who is ignorant, in whole or in part, of the true name of a person, partnership, firm or corporation which may properly be made a party defendant, may proceed against such defendant in any name used by the person, partnership, firm or corporation in conducting business, as defined in subdivision (a) of section eighteen hundred thirteen of this article.

(b) If the true name of the defendant becomes known at any time prior to the hearing on the merits, such information shall be brought to the attention of the clerk, who shall immediately amend all prior proceedings and papers. The clerk shall send an amended notice to the defendant, without payment of additional fees by the plaintiff, and all subsequent proceedings and papers shall be amended accordingly.

(c) In every action in the small claims part, at the hearing on the merits, the judge or arbitrator shall determine the defendant's true name. The clerk shall amend all prior proceedings and papers to conform to such determination, and all subsequent proceedings and papers shall be amended accordingly.

(d) A party against whom a judgment has been entered pursuant to this article, in any proceeding under section five thousand fifteen of the civil practice law and rules for relief from such judgment, shall, disclose its true name; any and all names in which it is conducting business; and any and all names in which it was conducting business at the time of the transaction or occurrence on which such judgment is based. All subsequent proceedings and papers shall be amended to conform to such disclosure.

§ 1815. Appearance by non-attorney representatives.

The court may permit, upon the request of a party, that a non-attorney representative, who is related by consanguinity or affinity to such party, be allowed to appear on behalf of such party when the court finds that due to the age, mental or physical capacity or other disability of such party that it is in the interests of justice to permit such representation. No person acting as a non-attorney representative shall be permitted to charge a fee or be allowed to accept any form of remuneration for such services.

Appendix F

Excerpt from the Uniform Civil Rules for the New York City Civil Court

§ 208.41. Small claims procedure.

1. (a) A small claims action shall be instituted by a plaintiff or someone on his or her behalf paying the filing fee as provided in NYCCCA 1803, and by supplying to the clerk the following information:

   (1) plaintiff's name and residence address;
   (2) defendant's name and place of residence, or place of business or employment; and
   (3) the nature and amount of the plaintiff's claim, giving dates and other relevant information.

(b) The clerk shall reduce this information to a written statement on a form provided therefor and shall record it in his or her office. The statement shall be in nontechnical, concise and simple language, and shall be signed by the person who shall have supplied the information contained therein.

(c) The clerk shall give to the person who signed the statement a memorandum of the time and place set for the hearing, which shall be as soon as practicable, and shall advise such person to produce at the hearing the supporting witnesses, account books, receipts or other documents required to establish the claim.

(d) Within five days after the action is recorded, the clerk shall send to the defendant by ordinary first class mail and by certified mail, return receipt requested, addressed to one or more of the addresses supplied as shall be deemed necessary, a signed notice bearing the seal of the court, which shall be in substantially the following form:

CIVIL COURT OF THE CITY OF NEW YORK
COUNTY OF _____
SMALL CLAIMS PART
TO:

_____

Take Notice that........................asks judgment in
this Court against you for $ ____, together with costs, upon
the following claim:

_____

_____

_____

There will be a hearing before the Court upon this claim
on____ , 19____, at ____ o'clock ____ M., in the Small
Claims Part, held at_____

You must appear and present your defense and any
counterclaim you may desire to assert at the hearing at the
time and place above set forth (a corporation must be
represented by an attorney or any authorized officer,
director or employee). IF YOU DO NOT APPEAR,
JUDGMENT WILL BE ENTERED AGAINST YOU BY
DEFAULT EVEN THOUGH YOU MAY HAVE A VALID
DEFENSE. If your defense or counterclaim, if any, is
supported by witnesses, account books, receipts or other
documents, you must produce them at the hearing. The
Clerk, if requested, will issue subpoenas for witnesses,
without fee thereof.

If you wish to present a counterclaim against the claimant, you must do so by filing with the Clerk of the Court a statement containing such counterclaim within five days of receiving this notice of claim. At the time of such filing you must pay the Clerk a filing fee of $3.00 plus the cost of postage to send your counterclaim by first class mail to the claimant. If you fail to file a counterclaim within this five-day period, you retain the right to file the counterclaim until the time of the hearing, but the claimant may request and obtain an adjournment of the hearing to a later date.

If you admit the claim, but desire time to pay, you must appear personally on the day set for the hearing and state to the Court your reasons for desiring time to pay.

Dated: _____, 20_____

_____
              Clerk

A Guide to Small Claims Court is available at the court listed above.

NOTE: If you desire a jury trial, you must, before the day upon which you have been notified to appear, file with the Clerk of the Court a written demand for a trial by jury. You must also pay to the clerk a jury fee of $55 and file an undertaking in the sum of $50 or deposit such sum in cash to secure the payment of any costs that may be awarded against you. You will also be required to make an affidavit specifying the issues of fact which you desire to have tried by a jury and stating that such trial is desired and demanded in good faith.

Under the law, the Court may award $25 additional costs to the plaintiff if a jury trial is demanded by you and a decision is rendered against you.

(e) The clerk shall note, on the statement referred to in subdivision (a) of this section, the date on which the notice was mailed and the address, the date of delivery shown by the return receipt and the name of the addressee or agent signing the receipt.

(f) Where all parties appear by attorneys, the case may be transferred to the appropriate county division of the Civil Court of the City of New York, and the claimant shall pay any additional filing fees required by law. If the claimant fails or refuses to pay such filing fees, the court shall dismiss the case.

(g) If service of notice cannot be effected upon the defendant within four months following the date on which the action was first instituted, the action shall be dismissed without prejudice.

(h) Unless the court shall otherwise order, a defendant to whom notice was duly given who fails to appear at the hearing on the day and time fixed, either in person or by attorney, shall be held to be in default, except that no default shall be ordered if the defendant or his attorney appear within one hour after the time fixed.

(i) If at the hearing it shall appear that the defendant has a counterclaim in an amount within the jurisdiction of the part for the hearing of small claims, the judge may either proceed forthwith to hear the entire case or may adjourn the hearing for a period of not more than 20 days, or as soon thereafter as may be practicable, at which adjourned time the hearing of the entire case shall be had. An adjournment shall be granted at the request of the claimant if the defendant did not file the counterclaim with the court within five days of receiving the notice of claim.

(j) An oath or affirmation shall be administered to all witnesses. The court shall conduct the hearing in such manner as it deems best suited to discover the facts and to determine the justice of the case. If the plaintiff, or an attorney in his or her behalf, does not appear at the time set for hearing, the court may dismiss the claim for want of prosecution or enter a finding on the merits for the defendant, or make such other disposition as it may deem proper.

(k) Where, after a claim is filed with the clerk, either party to the action desires to implead one or more additional defendants, the clerk shall, upon receipt of the proper fees, issue and mail a notice of claim to each additional defendant under the procedure set forth above.

(l) The undertaking to be filed by a defendant desiring a jury trial shall be in the form prescribed by the relevant provisions of article 25 of the CPLR.

(m) All motions pertaining to small claims shall be made returnable at a part and session appointed for the hearing of small claims, except that a motion to remove a case from the small claims part shall be made returnable in the appropriate motion part in the county division of the court in which the action is pending, and shall be in accord with the rules of the NYCCCA generally applicable to motion practice.

(n) There May be Arbitration of Any Small Claims Controversy.

> (1) The parties to any controversy, except infants and incompetents, may submit the same for arbitration to any attorney, duly appointed as a small claims arbitrator by the administrative judge of this court, so assigned for such duty at that term of the court and upon whom they shall agree.

> (2) The parties shall sign a consent which shall contain the name of the arbitrator, a brief recital of the nature of the controversy to be determined, a statement that they will abide by these rules, and an affirmation that the decision of the arbitrator is final and that no appeal shall lie from the award. The consent must be filed with the clerk of the small claims part.

> (3) The arbitrator shall forthwith proceed to hear the controversy. He or she shall not be bound by the rules regarding the admissibility of evidence, but all testimony shall be given under oath or affirmation. Either party may be represented by counsel, but no record of the proceeding before the arbitrator shall be

kept. No expense shall be incurred by the arbitrator except upon the consent in writing of the parties.

(4) After the first hearing, neither party may withdraw from the arbitration unless both parties consent to, or the arbitrator directs, a discontinuance of the proceeding.

(5) The arbitrator shall make an award in writing and file the same forthwith, together with his or her opinion, if any, with the clerk of the small claims part. Unless both parties file a request in writing not to enter judgment, the clerk shall, within two days after the filing of the award, enter judgment in accordance therewith, provided the award has been filed within 30 days from the date of filing the consent. The time within which the clerk shall enter judgment may be extended by a stipulation in writing for a further period not to exceed 30 days.

(6) No fees or disbursements of any kind shall be demanded or received except as hereinabove provided.

Appendix G

Excerpt from New York Civil Practice Law and Rules

§ 1209. Arbitration of controversy involving infant, judicially declared incompetent or conservatee.

A controversy involving an infant, person judicially declared to be incompetent or conservatee shall not be submitted to arbitration except pursuant to a court order made upon application of the representative of such infant, incompetent or conservatee; provided, however, that a claim brought on behalf of an infant pursuant to paragraph one or two of subdivision (f) of section three thousand four hundred twenty of the insurance law may be submitted to arbitration without a court order.

§ 3015 (e). License to do business.

Where the plaintiff's cause of action against a consumer arises from the plaintiff's conduct of a business which is required by state or local law to be licensed by the department of consumer affairs of the city of New York, the Suffolk county department of consumer affairs, the Westchester county department of consumer affairs/weight-measures, the county of Rockland, the county of Putnam or the Nassau county department of consumer affairs, the complaint shall allege, as part of the cause of action, that plaintiff is duly licensed and shall contain the name and number, if any, of such license and the governmental agency which issued such license; provided, however, that where the plaintiff does not have a license at the commencement of the action the plaintiff may, subject to the provisions of rule thirty hundred twenty-five of this article, amend the complaint with the name and number of an after-acquired license and the name of the governmental agency which issued such license or move for leave to amend the complaint in accordance with such provisions. The failure of the plaintiff to comply with this subdivision will permit the defendant to move for dismissal pursuant to paragraph seven of subdivision (a) of rule thirty-two hundred eleven of this chapter.

§ 5205. Personal property exempt from application to the satisfaction of money judgments.

(a) Exemption for personal property. The following personal property when owned by any person is exempt from application to the satisfaction of a money judgment except where the judgment is for the purchase price of the exempt property or was recovered by a domestic, laboring person or mechanic for work performed by that person in such capacity:

1. all stoves and home heating equipment kept for use in the judgment debtor's dwelling house and necessary fuel therefor for one hundred twenty days; one sewing machine with its appurtenances;

2. religious texts, family pictures and portraits, and school books used by the judgment debtor or in the family; and other books, not exceeding five hundred dollars in value, kept and used as part of the family or judgment debtor's library;

3. a seat or pew occupied by the judgment debtor or the family in a place of public worship;

4. domestic animals with the necessary food for those animals for one hundred twenty days, provided that the total value of such animals and food does not exceed one thousand dollars; all necessary food actually provided for the use of the judgment debtor or his family for one hundred twenty days;

5. all wearing apparel, household furniture, one mechanical, gas or electric refrigerator, one radio receiver, one television set, one computer and associated equipment, one cellphone, crockery, tableware and cooking utensils necessary for the judgment debtor and the family; all prescribed health aids;

6. a wedding ring; a watch, jewelry and art not exceeding one thousand dollars in value;

7. tools of trade necessary working tools and implements, including those of a mechanic, farm machinery, team, professional instruments, furniture and library, not exceeding three thousand dollars in value, together with the necessary

food for the team for one hundred twenty days, provided, however, that the articles specified in this paragraph are necessary to the carrying on of the judgment debtor's profession or calling;

8. one motor vehicle not exceeding four thousand dollars in value above liens and encumbrances of the debtor; if such vehicle has been equipped for use by a disabled debtor, then ten thousand dollars in value above liens and encumbrances of the debtor; provided, however, that this exemption for one motor vehicle shall not apply if the debt enforced is for child support, spousal support, maintenance, alimony or equitable distribution; and

9. if no homestead exemption is claimed, then one thousand dollars in personal property, bank account or cash.

(b) Exemption of cause of action and damages for taking or injuring exempt personal property. A cause of action, to recover damages for taking or injuring personal property exempt from application to the satisfaction of a money judgment, is exempt from application to the satisfaction of a money judgment. A money judgment and its proceeds arising out of such a cause of action is exempt, for one year after the collection thereof, from application to the satisfaction of a money judgment.

(c) Trust exemption. 1. Except as provided in paragraphs four and five of this subdivision, all property while held in trust for a judgment debtor, where the trust has been created by, or the fund so held in trust has proceeded from, a person other than the judgment debtor, is exempt from application to the satisfaction of a money judgment.

2. For purposes of this subdivision, all trusts, custodial accounts, annuities, insurance contracts, monies, assets or interests established as part of, and all payments from, either any trust or plan, which is qualified as an individual retirement account under section four hundred eight or section four hundred eight A of the United States Internal Revenue Code of 1986, as amended, a Keogh (HR-10), retirement or other plan established by a corporation, which is qualified under section 401 of the United States Internal

Revenue Code of 1986, as amended, or created as a result of rollovers from such plans pursuant to sections 402 (a) (5), 403 (a) (4), 408 (d) (3) or 408A of the Internal Revenue Code of 1986, as amended, or a plan that satisfies the requirements of section 457 of the Internal Revenue Code of 1986, as amended, shall be considered a trust which has been created by or which has proceeded from a person other than the judgment debtor, even though such judgment debtor is (i) in the case of an individual retirement account plan, an individual who is the settlor of and depositor to such account plan, or (ii) a self-employed individual, or (iii) a partner of the entity sponsoring the Keogh (HR-10) plan, or (iv) a shareholder of the corporation sponsoring the retirement or other plan or (v) a participant in a section 457 plan.

3. All trusts, custodial accounts, annuities, insurance contracts, monies, assets, or interests described in paragraph two of this subdivision shall be conclusively presumed to be spendthrift trusts under this section and the common law of the state of New York for all purposes, including, but not limited to, all cases arising under or related to a case arising under sections one hundred one to thirteen hundred thirty of title eleven of the United States Bankruptcy Code, as amended.

4. This subdivision shall not impair any rights an individual has under a qualified domestic relations order as that term is defined in section 414(p) of the United States Internal Revenue Code of 1986, as amended or under any order of support, alimony or maintenance of any court of competent jurisdiction to enforce arrears/past due support whether or not such arrears/past due support have been reduced to a money judgment.

5. Additions to an asset described in paragraph two of this subdivision shall not be exempt from application to the satisfaction of a money judgment if (i) made after the date that is ninety days before the interposition of the claim on which such judgment was entered, or (ii) deemed to be fraudulent conveyances under article ten of the debtor and creditor law. (d) Income exemptions. The following personal

property is exempt from application to the satisfaction of a money judgment, except such part as a court determines to be unnecessary for the reasonable requirements of the judgment debtor and his dependents: 1. ninety per cent of the income or other payments from a trust the principal of which is exempt under subdivision (c); provided, however, that with respect to any income or payments made from trusts, custodial accounts, annuities, insurance contracts, monies, assets or interest established as part of an individual retirement account plan or as part of a Keogh (HR-10), retirement or other plan described in paragraph two of subdivision (c) of this section, the exception in this subdivision for such part as a court determines to be unnecessary for the reasonable requirements of the judgment debtor and his dependents shall not apply, and the ninety percent exclusion of this paragraph shall become a one hundred percent exclusion;

2. ninety per cent of the earnings of the judgment debtor for his personal services rendered within sixty days before, and at any time after, an income execution is delivered to the sheriff or a motion is made to secure the application of the judgment debtor's earnings to the satisfaction of the judgment; and

3. payments pursuant to an award in a matrimonial action, for the support of a wife, where the wife is the judgment debtor, or for the support of a child, where the child is the judgment debtor; where the award was made by a court of the state, determination of the extent to which it is unnecessary shall be made by that court.

(e) Exemptions to members of armed forces. The pay and bounty of a non-commissioned officer, musician or private in the armed forces of the United States or the state of New York; a land warrant, pension or other reward granted by the United States, or by a state, for services in the armed forces; a sword, horse, medal, emblem or device of any kind presented as a testimonial for services rendered in the armed forces of the United States or a state; and the uniform, arms and equipments which were used by a person in the service, are exempt from application to the satisfaction of a money judgment; provided, however, that the provisions of this subdivision shall not apply to the satisfaction of any order or money judgment for the support of a person's child, spouse, or former spouse.

(f) Exemption for unpaid milk proceeds. Ninety per cent of any money or debt due or to become due to the judgment debtor for the sale of milk produced on a farm operated by him and delivered for his account to a milk dealer licensed pursuant to article twenty-one of the agriculture and markets law is exempt from application to the satisfaction of a money judgment.

(g) Security deposit exemption. Money deposited as security for the rental of real property to be used as the residence of the judgment debtor or the judgment debtor's family; and money deposited as security with a gas, electric, water, steam, telegraph or telephone corporation, or a municipality rendering equivalent utility services, for services to judgment debtor's residence or the residence of judgment debtor's family, are exempt from application to the satisfaction of a money judgment.

(h) The following personal property is exempt from application to the satisfaction of money judgment, except such part as a court determines to be unnecessary for the reasonable requirements of the judgment debtor and his dependents:

1. any and all medical and dental accessions to the human body and all personal property or equipment that is necessary or proper to maintain or assist in sustaining or maintaining one or more major life activities or is utilized to provide mobility for a person with a permanent disability; and

2. any guide dog, service dog or hearing dog, as those terms are defined in section one hundred eight of the agriculture and markets law, or any animal trained to aid or assist a person with a permanent disability and actually being so used by such person, together with any and all food or feed for any such dog or other animal.

(i) Exemption for life insurance policies. The right of a judgment debtor to accelerate payment of part or all of the death benefit or special surrender value under a life insurance policy, as authorized by paragraph one of subsection (a) of section one thousand one hundred thirteen of the insurance law, or to enter into a viatical settlement pursuant to the provisions of article seventy-eight of the insurance law, is exempt from application to the satisfaction of a money judgment.

(j) Exemption for New York state college choice tuition savings program trust fund payment monies. Monies in an account created pursuant to article fourteen-A of the education law are exempt from application to the satisfaction of a money judgment as follows:

1. one hundred percent of monies in an account established in connection with a scholarship program established pursuant to such article is exempt;

2. one hundred percent of monies in an account is exempt where the judgment debtor is the account owner and designated beneficiary of such account and is a minor; and

3. an amount not exceeding ten thousand dollars in an account, or in the aggregate for more than one account, is exempt where the judgment debtor is the account owner of such account or accounts. For purposes of this subdivision, the terms "account owner" and "designated beneficiary" shall have the meanings ascribed to them in article fourteen-A of the education law.

(k) Notwithstanding any other provision of law to the contrary, where the judgment involves funds of a convicted person as defined in paragraph (c) of subdivision one of section six hundred thirty-two-a of the executive law, and all or a portion of such funds represent compensatory damages awarded by judgment to a convicted person in a separate action, a judgment obtained pursuant to such section six hundred thirty-two-a shall not be subject to execution or enforcement against the first ten percent of the portion of such funds that represents compensatory damages in the convicted person's action; provided, however, that this exemption from execution or enforcement shall not apply to judgments obtained by a convicted person prior to the effective date of the chapter of the laws of two thousand one which added this sentence or to any amendment to such judgment where such amendment was obtained on or after the effective date of this subdivision. For the purpose of determining the amount of a judgment which is not subject to execution or enforcement pursuant to this subdivision: (i) the court shall deduct attorney's fees from that portion of the judgment that represents compensatory damages and multiply the remainder of compensatory damages by ten percent; and (ii) when the judgment includes compensatory and punitive damages, attorney's fees shall be prorated among compensatory and punitive damages in the same proportion that all attorney's fees bear to all damages recovered.

§ 5206. Real property exempt from application to the satisfaction of money judgments.

(a) Exemption of homestead. Property of one of the following types, not exceeding one hundred fifty thousand dollars for the counties of Kings, Queens, New York, Bronx, Richmond, Nassau, Suffolk, Rockland, Westchester and Putnam; one hundred twenty-five thousand dollars for the counties of Dutchess, Albany, Columbia, Orange, Saratoga and Ulster; and seventy-five thousand dollars for the remaining counties of the state in value above liens and encumbrances, owned and occupied as a principal residence, is exempt from application to the satisfaction of a money judgment, unless the judgment was recovered wholly for the purchase price thereof:

1. a lot of land with a dwelling thereon,
2. shares of stock in a cooperative apartment corporation,
3. units of a condominium apartment, or
4. a mobile home.

But no exempt homestead shall be exempt from taxation or from sale for non-payment of taxes or assessments.

(b) Homestead exemption after owner's death. The homestead exemption continues after the death of the person in whose favor the property was exempted for the benefit of the surviving spouse and surviving children until the majority of the youngest surviving child and until the death of the surviving spouse.

(c) Suspension of occupation as affecting homestead. The homestead exemption ceases if the property ceases to be occupied as a residence by a person for whose benefit it may so continue, except where the suspension of occupation is for a period not exceeding one year, and occurs in consequence of injury to, or destruction of, the dwelling house upon the premises.

(d) Exemption of homestead exceeding one hundred fifty thousand dollars in value for the counties of Kings, Queens, New York, Bronx, Richmond, Nassau, Suffolk, Rockland, Westchester and Putnam; one hundred twenty-five thousand dollars for the counties of Dutchess, Albany, Columbia, Orange, Saratoga and Ulster; and seventy-five thousand dollars for the remaining counties of the state. The exemption of a homestead is not void because the value of the property exceeds one hundred fifty thousand dollars for the counties of Kings, Queens, New York, Bronx, Richmond, Nassau, Suffolk, Rockland, Westchester and Putnam; one hundred twenty-five thousand dollars for the counties of Dutchess, Albany, Columbia, Orange, Saratoga and Ulster; and seventy-five thousand dollars for the remaining counties of the state but the lien of a judgment attaches to the surplus.

(e) Sale of homestead exceeding one hundred fifty thousand dollars for the counties of Kings, Queens, New York, Bronx, Richmond, Nassau, Suffolk, Rockland, Westchester and Putnam; one hundred twenty-five thousand dollars for the counties of Dutchess, Albany, Columbia, Orange, Saratoga and Ulster; and seventy-five thousand dollars for the remaining counties of the state in value. A judgment creditor may commence a special proceeding in the county in which the homestead is located against the judgment debtor for the sale, by a sheriff or receiver, of a homestead exceeding ten thousand dollars in value. The court may direct that the notice of petition be served upon any other person. The court, if it directs such a sale, shall so marshal the proceeds of the sale that the right and interest of each person in the proceeds shall correspond as nearly as may be to his right and interest in the property sold. Money, not exceeding one hundred fifty thousand dollars for the counties of Kings, Queens, New York, Bronx, Richmond, Nassau, Suffolk, Rockland, Westchester and Putnam; one hundred twenty-five thousand dollars for the counties of Dutchess, Albany, Columbia, Orange, Saratoga and Ulster; and seventy-five thousand dollars for the remaining counties of the state, paid to a judgment debtor, as representing his interest in the proceeds, is exempt for one year after the payment, unless, before the expiration of the year, he acquires an exempt homestead, in which case, the exemption ceases with respect to so much of the money as was not expended for the purchase of that property; and the exemption of the property so acquired extends to every debt against which the property sold was exempt. Where the exemption of property sold as prescribed in this subdivision has been continued after the judgment debtor's death, or where he dies after the sale and before payment to him of his portion of the proceeds of the sale, the court may direct that portion of the proceeds which represents his interest be invested for the benefit of the person or persons entitled to the benefit of the exemption, or be otherwise disposed of as justice requires.

(f) Exemption of burying ground. Land, set apart as a family or private burying ground, is exempt from application to the satisfaction of a money judgment, upon the following conditions only:

1. a portion of it must have been actually used for that purpose;

2. it must not exceed in extent one-fourth of an acre; and

3. it must not contain any building or structure, except one or more vaults or other places of deposit for the dead, or mortuary monuments.

Appendix H

Small Claims Complaint Form
New York City Civil Court

CIVIL COURT OF THE CITY OF NEW YORK
SMALL CLAIMS PART
STATEMENT OF CLAIM

(FOR OFFICE USE ONLY)

INSTRUCTIONS:
Place only ONE letter or number in each space
and leave a blank space between words.

(You)

I. CLAIMANT'S INFORMATION

LAST NAME

FIRST NAME   MIDDLE INITIAL

ADDRESS
(NO P O BOX)

BOROUGH, CITY,   STATE   ZIP
TOWN OR VILL.

OTHER INFO
[Doing Business As] [In Care Of]
[Attention To] Circle One

PHONE NO.

(They)

II. DEFENDANT'S INFORMATION*

LAST NAME
(or Full Business Name)

FIRST NAME   MIDDLE INITIAL

ADDRESS
(NO P O BOX)

BOROUGH CITY,   STATE N Y ZIP
TOWN. OR VILL.

OTHER INFO
[Doing Business As] [In Care Of]
[Attention To] Circle One

PHONE NO.

III. CLAIM

Amount Claimed $ (Maximum $5,000)   Date of Occurrence or Transaction

Place of occurrence, if Auto Accident

PRIMARY REASON FOR CLAIM (Check One):

Damage caused to:	automobile	other personal property	real property	person
Failure to provide:	proper repairs	proper services	proper merchandise	goods paid for
Failure to return:	security	property	deposit	money loaned
Failure to pay:	salary	for services rendered	insurance claim	
	rent	commissions	for goods sold and delivered	agreement
Breach of:	contract	lease	warranty	use of property
Loss of:	luggage	property	time from work	
Returned:	check (bounced)	check (stopped)		
Other: (Be brief)				

IDENTIFYING NUMBER(S) - (Receipt #, Claim #, Account #, Policy #, Ticket #, License #, Plate #'(s))

Today's Date   **Signature of Claimant or Agent**

* DEFENDANT'S NAME: The **legal** name will be required in order to obtain an enforceable judgment. If the Defendant is a **business**, its full and correct **business name** should be obtained from the Office of the County Clerk in the county in which the business is located or check on the following website: **www.dos.state.ny.us**
DEFENDANT'S ADDRESS: YOU must indicate the proper street address of the Defendant. A Post Office Box is not acceptable.

NOTE: If the Claim is a result of an automobile accident, the Claim must be OWNER against OWNER.

CIV-SC-50 (Revised 7/05)

CERT'D #

COA CODE

CLAIM AMT.
$

FEE
STANDARD FEE
☐ CLAIMANT V. DEFENDANT
NO FEE
☐ DEFENDANT V. THIRD PARTY
☐ CLAIMANT V. ADD'L DEFENDANT
☐ POSTAGE ONLY
☐ WAGE CLAIM TO $300

LANGUAGE

DATE DATA ENTERED

DATE NOTICES MAILED

CASE TYPE:
MULTI DFT ☐   CTRCLM ☐
3 PARTY ☐   CRS/CMPLT ☐

FIRST DATE

DAY COURT
☐ STATUTORY ☐ OTHER
FREE CIVIL COURT FORM
So fee may be charged to fill in this form.
Form can be found at
http://www.nycourts.gov/courts/nyc/smallclaims/forms.shtml

Glossary

adjournment	Delay until another time.
assignee	Grantee, one to whom an assignment is made.
assignment	Act of transferring a property interest or cause of action to another.
bar	(1) Restriction, exclusion, prohibition, as, a bar to prosecution of an action; (2) railing in a courtroom to separate judge, jury, counsel and parties from the public; (3) body of members of the legal profession; (4) "at bar", meaning before the court.
breach of contract	Failure to comply with terms of a contract.
claimant	One who asserts a right or title.
conservatee	a person whom a court has determined because of physical or mental limitations or old age requires a conservator to handle his/her financial affairs, and/or his/her actual personal activities such as arranging a residence, health care and the like.
consolidation	Union of several into one.
cross-claim	Claim made by a defendant against a plaintiff or against a co-defendant, concerning matters in controversy in the original proceeding.
damage	Loss due to harm, injury or deterioration.

defendant	A person against whom a court action is initiated.
discovery	(1) Pre-trial process by which a party to an action secures information from his opponent as to facts or documents in the opponent's possession or control; (2) revelation, disclosure, recognition.
execution of judgment	Process by which order of court is put into effect.
hearsay	Generally, information heard from someone else, as opposed to information based on personal observation or knowledge.
implead	Include in an action between other persons.
incompetent (n.)	(1) one who is unable to manage his own affairs by reason of insanity, imbecility or other mental condition as defined by statute; (2) one incapable of doing what is required.
infant	Person under age of majority, as defined by statute.
liability	Obligation, debt, burden, drawback.
mediation	Intervention by a third person to settle or reconcile a controversy between conflicting parties.
merchant	One engaged in business of buying and selling goods.
plaintiff	A person who initiates a court action.
pro se	For himself.

referee	Officer having power conferred by a court to examine a controversy, take testimony, determine facts, and make a report and recommendation to the court.
statute of frauds	Legislation of common law origin requiring certain documents to be in writing and signed by the party to be charged, thereby minimizing opportunity for fraud or perjury.
stay of execution	The stopping by a court of the carrying out or implementation of a judgment, that is, of a court order previously issued.
subpoena	A written order issued by a judicial officer, prosecutor, defense attorney or grand jury, requiring a specified person to appear in a designated court at a specified time in order to testify in a case under the jurisdiction of that court, or to bring material to be used as evidence to that court.
subpoena duces tecum	Legal process requiring one to appear as a witness, and bring with him specified books and records in his possession.
tort	Wrongful act or breach of legal duty resulting in damage, not founded on contract.
vacate	To set aside, render void, empty.
vicarious	Serving in place of something original, acting as a substitute.

Index